# THE

# COBURN

NORTHERN CALIFORNIA'S UNSOLVED MURDER

# MYSTERY

BY

## JUNE MORRALL

*To the village in the middle of nowhere...*

Birds Eye View
of
San Mateo
County
California
showing
Boulevards
and connecting
Automobile
Roads

© 1992 June Morrall

**Library of Congress Cataloging in Publication Data:**

Morrall, June
The Coburn Mystery: Northern California's Unsolved Murder

1. Pescadero — History
2. San Mateo County — History
3. Northern California — History
Library of Congress Catalog No. 92-081071
ISBN 0-9602088-1-X

Published by
**Moonbeam Press**
P.O. Box 802
El Granada CA 94018

Cover and book design by **Jim Rudolph** — **WaterWork Art** San Francisco

# PROLOGUE

For over sixty years millionaire landowner Loren Coburn was feared and despised by his Pescadero neighbors. The Coburn saga did not end with his death as a victim of the 1918 Influenza Pandemic, but it climaxed in a seamy mystery. In its wake there was stony silence, and an unwritten pact to suppress the ghosts.

When the day came that all the significant players in the Coburn drama had died or moved away, the Pescaderans breathed a sigh of relief and pushed the events deep into the recesses of their collective memories. The mystery was still there, but the bizarre story was not shared with outsiders.

As I unpeeled the layers of this complex story, I was frustrated. My surviving sources were children at the time the strange events unfolded. While very helpful, their recollections could not give me a complete compass of the chilling Coburn mystery.

After hundreds of hours digging through newspaper archives and court records and after countless deadends and unanswered letters, I have exposed the fascinating true story that lay dormant in a tiny, remote village by the ocean.

# ACKNOWLEDGMENTS

*I am grateful to Mrs. Caroline Dias, George and Jessie Davis, Joe and Grace Duarte, and Mrs. Jean Machado for coloring in the background of this fascinating story. Their memories provided a vivid picture of the main characters.*

*Thank you, Ron Duarte, for introducing me to your charming aunt.*

*My deepest appreciation goes to my editor, Luana Hammett.*

*This book would not be possible without the existence of the San Mateo County Historical Museum. I am indebted to Executive Director Mitch Postel and Archivist Marion Holmes, both of whom have always made their resources available. I would not have stumbled upon this story had I not been rummaging through the museum's files, including the Kenneth McCready manuscript.*

*This book could not have been written without the help of experts. Thank you Ken R. LaJoie, from the United States Geological Survey, for the time you took to answer my many questions about Pebble Beach.*

*The assistance of excellent reference librarians made all the difference in my quest for information. I am grateful to Sylvia Bender-Lamb, California Division of Mines and Geology, Barney Bloom of the Vermont Historical Society, Annette Dolode, Holyoke Library, and Meg Welden, Historical Coordinator for the Monterey County Parks. Mona Gudgel, who directs the Monterey County Historical Society, welcomed me and helped in every way she could when I visited her at the Boronda Adobe.*

*A big thank you to Vicky Dulaney at the California State Library for her immediate response to my requests.*

*Other extremely helpful sources were: Suzanne Locke of the San Francisco Examiner, Richard Ogar of the Bancroft Library, and photo researcher Lindsey Kefauver. Sacramento researcher Nancy Morebeck, Judy Lavelle, and Monterey County resident Jim Pettitt were also very helpful.*

*Jeremy Voas, the publisher and editor of the* Half Moon Bay Review *was very supportive. Some of my early stories about Loren Coburn and Pescadero appeared in my "Coastside Memories" column.*

*My thanks to coastside resident Jim Rudolph of Waterwork Art in San Francisco, who designed the book cover and conceived the book's format. Thank you Brenda Phillips for making all the manuscript changes so cheerfully.*

*My parents, Charles and Catherine Martin were always there for me.*

*Thank you Doreen Pecoraro, who works at the U.S. Post Office in El Granada, for constantly asking me when this book was going to be finished!*

*And, to Burt with love.*

# THE COBURN MYSTERY

## PART IV — VARIOUS COURT CASES

## PART V — THE NEWCOMERS

## FINAL WORDS
## EPILOGUE

*In 1919 when the troops were coming home, Pescadero—which means "fishing place"—was an isolated rural farming community.*

*Although it was only forty miles south of San Francisco on the San Mateo County Coastside, and a shorter distance from the county government seat on the other side of the mountains, the roads were primitive. The population hovered around one thousand. However, jobs, even in farming, were scarce. The people were poor, and the community seemed to be closed to outsiders.*

# PART I

## LIFE IN PESCADERO

Courtesy: *San Mateo County Historical Association*

# CHAPTER ONE

# A MURDER

*Many years later, locals, who had been youngsters in 1919,
remembered the official cars parked in front of the Coburn house on San
Gregorio Street and recalled that they were told to stay away. Everyone
seemed to be frightened in Pescadero.*

A crowd of police, private detectives, and curious onlookers milled
around the dreary Loren Coburn house on Wednesday, June 4, 1919.
One of the responsibilities of San Mateo County Sheriff Michael Sheehan
was to discourage anyone from disrupting the investigation. Known as
"the terror of criminals", Sheehan had more than once used his muscular
physique to bar the way.

A key witness was Joe Quilla, Mrs. Sarah Coburn's Portuguese-
speaking ranchhand. Quilla, who had milked the three cows in the
pasture behind the house at 7:30 a.m., said that the day began like any
other—but then it took an unexpected twist.

It was 8 a.m. when he followed his daily chores and went to deliver a
bucket of fresh milk to the wealthy widow. He knocked on the back door,
and, for the first time that he could remember, no one answered. Clearly
something was wrong. Either Mrs. Coburn or Mrs. Harrison, the housekeeper
who had been hired a year ago, should have come to the door promptly.

Quilla tapped on the bedroom window, and he pressed his face
against the cool glass. The shades were drawn. There was no response
from within the house. Without actually seeing it, he said that he knew a
tiny light emanated from the coal-oil lamp beside Sarah's bed, because
she always kept it lit.

He was frightened when he heard the familiar mumbling on the opposite side of the window; this would be from Sarah's sixty-three-year-old stepson Wally, known as "the boy" to the villagers.

Spooked, Quilla ran for help. It wasn't far from the house to the road. On the other side of San Gregorio Street he spotted Sarah's trusted friend, Andy Stirling, wearing riding breeches and joshing with a villager in front of the candy and tobacco store called the Emporium. It was a small, narrow, wooden structure that paled beside San Francisco's big Emporium.

Carl Coburn, a former County Supervisor in his early thirties, owned the little Emporium. He had left Pescadero at 6 a.m. that morning for Redwood City, on business, a trip that took him east over the mountain ridge. He was the "adopted son" of Sarah and Loren Coburn, a replacement for Loren's own son, Wally, who was demented. Loren Coburn, the eccentric landowner, had died only seven months earlier during the influenza epidemic, at age ninety-two, after a long and stormy relationship with the villagers.

Andy Stirling was a powerfully built man in his late thirties. He was a personable fellow who had endeared himself to Sarah. Everybody liked him when he was sober, but he lost his charm when he drank too much. Stirling worked for Christian ("Chris") H. Widemann, who leased ten thousand acres of the breathtakingly beautiful Coburn land. The ranch property that spread like fingers away from the Pacific Ocean was rented out and cultivated. The grandson of a rich merchant, Widemann had come north from Monterey County and started a goat-milk facility, a great boon for the isolated community in need of jobs. Widemann was hoping to cash in on the use of goat milk as a cure for tuberculosis.

Stirling showed concern for what Sarah's nervous Portuguese ranchhand told him, and the two men walked briskly across the road to the old Coburn house. An experienced ex-deputy sheriff from Monterey County, Stirling was surprised to find the front door open. He knew that Sarah locked the front door every night and that she placed a chair against it as well. The chair was gone.

The wooden floor creaked and groaned as the men rushed to the back of the house to Sarah's bedroom. To the immediate right of the door the coal-oil lamp burned solemnly.

The next events happened quickly.

Stirling saw Sarah Satira Coburn's body "...lying partially robed on her bed. Her head was crushed and bleeding...," he told a reporter from the *San Francisco News*. Dried blood coated her nose and mouth. The white bed sheets were stained red. Sprays of blood splattered across one wall. As his vision absorbed more of the room and his mind made sense out of what he saw, Stirling expected to see overturned furniture. But there was no evidence of a struggle.

When the demented stepson who lived in the house suddenly veered into the room, Stirling tensed. Wearing a long, white nightshirt, Wallace Loren Coburn was a nice looking man, tall and slender, endowed with the fair skin of his father. His unkempt hair was dark, and he wore a beard. Disoriented, distraught, and muttering incoherently, Wally began to pace the bedroom floor in a peripatetic manner. He was an old man, but fate had cheated him out of a normal life by cursing him with the mind of a child.

"Wallace refused to answer any questions...," said Stirling. "He simply folded his hands behind his back and walked up and down in the circle we made around him..."

Then "the boy" dropped to his knees. With a wrinkled brow, he looked as if he might pray at the side of his dead stepmother's body. According to Quilla and Stirling, Wally shook her body roughly and then abruptly caressed her.

"...I spoke to him," said Stirling, "but he did not reply other than to fly into a fit of rage and shake the body again..." Stirling claimed to hear Wally "growl...like an animal." When he leaned over his stepmother's body, he whispered softly to her, calling her Aunt Satira. He shook the dead woman imploring: "Wake up sweetheart, wake up sweetheart... Sweetheart, ain't you going to get up?"

The shock of seeing Sarah Coburn's dead body finally spurred Andy Stirling into action. He telephoned Dr. Clarence Victor Thompson, the handsome and dapper thiry-eight-year-old physician and County Supervisor, who lived around the corner. He also telephoned the County Sheriff's office; news of the murder was out. All the calls had to be routed through the switchboard located in McCormick's general store.

Leaving Wally with the ranchhand, Stirling went outside to round up more help from the neighbors and to wire news of the murder to a Monterey County judge, a close friend of the victim. "When I returned," Stirling said, "we got Wallace out of the room. He quieted down and let us search him..." The men seized a butcher knife in Wally's room, which adjoined Sarah's room—but there were no visible knife wounds on Sarah's body.

Dr. Thompson pronounced that Mrs. Coburn had been dead for several hours; there would be an official coroner's inquiry later that day. The doctor helped Wally change into the cast-off clothing that had belonged to his father. Someone put a white carnation in the lapel of his oversized jacket. His long hair, that people said had not been cut by a barber for forty-five years, was pulled away from his face and knotted into a braid. A bowler hat was placed on his head.

Then Andy Stirling discovered the possible murder weapon: a wooden club two feet long and three inches wide. It lay on the floor in the hallway between Sarah's and Wally's bedrooms. Quilla recognized the weapon at once: it was part of a load of firewood that he had carried into the house the day before. The bloodstained club, probably marked with fingerprints, could have solved the mystery of who murdered Mrs. Coburn. Stirling picked it up to feel its weight and handed it to the ranchhand, who handed it to Dr. Thompson, who passed it around to the other men present. The men observed that there were no traces of blood on Wally's white nightgown, yet they said that their gut feelings were that "the boy" did it; he was the only other person in the house.

Until the authorities got there, what were they going to do with "the boy"? Andy Stirling asked Joe Quilla to take Wally to his own house, but he soon returned, because Mrs. Quilla, who did occasional housework for Mrs. Coburn and knew Wally, refused to take responsibility for "the boy's" safety. So Wally waited for the sheriff in the Coburn house.

With one of the men watching "the boy", Andy slipped out. As he walked to McCormick's General Store, he met Frank "Kid" Zug, a small-time pugilist from 'back East'. Kid Zug, whose face was battered from his many bouts in the ring, worked as a house painter for Chris Widemann, the big employer in Pescadero. Stirling told Zug that the old lady was dead.

The telephone was ringing when they walked into McCormick's store. Nobody was around to answer it, so Zug nudged Stirling, who was uncharacteristically agitated, to answer it. Finally Stirling took the old-fashioned receiver down and talked into the telephone. Since McCormick's was a general store and a place where gossip originated, it was not a surprise that a San Francisco reporter was on the line. The reporter asked Stirling for confirmation that Sarah Coburn had been murdered. "Yes", said Stirling; and, he added, with the knowledge of an insider, "it looked as if the stepson, Wally, did it."

The news of the murder was flashed to San Francisco Chief of Police White, Duncan Matheson, Chief of the San Francisco Detective Bureau, San Mateo County Sheriff Michael Sheehan, and San Mateo County District Attorney Franklin Swart.

Swart had been reelected District Attorney by a large majority, but his political enemies charged that he and Sheriff Sheehan had not done enough to close illegal gambling dens. It was alleged that these places were fleecing United States soldiers while they played pedro and poker at the Northern Club and the Villa Mateo. A grand jury investigation turned up nothing, but the damage to the politically ambitious District Attorney Swart had been done.

He hoped that the sensational Inez Reed murder trial could repair the damage and advance his career—if he could convict Dr. Northcott, the defendant. The case of Inez Reed, an Army nurse, drew much sympathy, and the public was horrified by her murder. The newspapers had covered the story faithfully, and jury selection in the bungled abortion case was scheduled to begin in a few days.

Now Swart would have to break away from the Inez Reed case to investigate an equally headline-grabbing murder. In contrast to the young woman, the new victim, Sarah Coburn, was the rich, eighty-three-year-old widow of an eccentric landowner.

The District Attorney knew the Coburn name very well; few people in San Mateo County did not know the name. For years the strange events surrounding the Coburns's private and public life had escalated, providing fertile seeds of gossip.

Loren Coburn had earned the dubious distinction of being the most litigious individual in the county; the courtroom became his second home. It was not even a profitable place for the many attorneys who represented the millionaire, because Loren Coburn was penurious and frequently balked at paying the attorneys, who often had to sue in order to collect their fees.

Sarah Coburn's murder came at an inopportune moment for the overworked San Mateo County District Attorney: The San Francisco police were looking into the Inez Reed murder, and Captain Duncan Matheson would be sitting next to him in court, crowding him, breathing down his neck. There was a fierce rivalry with the San Francisco Police, who considered themselves superior to their San Mateo County counterparts. Police Chief White was not shy about voicing his grievances regarding what he considered lack of progress in the critical, early days of the Inez Reed case.

"If we can get the body [of Inez Reed], I am sure we can solve the mystery," boasted White. Her body was in possession of the San Mateo County authorities.

It was not only the San Francisco Police who taunted Swart and the San Mateo County Police force. San Francisco's ruthless District Attorney, Matthew Brady, latched onto any case that showed promise of publicity.

Sheriff Sheehan, who had also been stung by allegations that he had not done his job and shut down illegal gambling, motored with Swart over the scenic, forested mountain ridge that separated Redwood City from

Pescadero. Police Chief White traveled to the murder scene with two detectives. They careened along the single-lane, unpaved road that threaded through the mountains into the pretty Pescadero valley. The automobile was still new enough that the newspapers reported on the motor trip that formerly had taken hours by stagecoach.

San Gregorio Street was dusty, not more than one block long, fronted by wooden buildings, saloons, stables, general stores, an old hotel, and the Coburn house, partially obscured by a pair of gnarled trees. A flower garden and neat rows of fava beans were planted in the front yard, hardly the house of a millionaire.

After meeting with witnesses Quilla and Stirling, Swart, who arrived before the San Francisco Police, learned that the front door was unlocked when the body of Mrs. Coburn was found. In a small village where everyone was known—and where unlocked doors must have been common—what did she fear so much that she not only locked the door, but always leaned a chair against it?

The District Attorney asked for the whereabouts of Mrs. Harrison, the housekeeper, and was told she had gone to San Francisco on a shopping trip the day before.

Inside the house that smelled of old age, Swart met County Coroner William Ansyl Brooke. Well-liked, Dr. Brooke had come to the San Mateo County Coastside as a physician with the Ocean Shore Railroad. This was the famous "reaches the beaches" railroad that hugged the cliffs above the Pacific Ocean and offered tourists and commuters a thrilling ride from San Francisco to Tunitas Creek, north of Pescadero.

The coroner told Swart that Dr. Thompson was in the bedroom with the body. In fact, in a departure from the usual procedure, Dr. Thompson was going to perform the autopsy in the room.

The officials appraised the Coburns's cheaply-furnished house. Their eyes glanced over the faded carpets and the third-rate furniture. The Coburns were supposedly rich, but their surroundings reflected neither wealth nor materialism. What did they do with their money during all these years?

The big safe that occupied a corner in the dingy dining room was a tempting object. It was known that Loren Coburn, who was proud to say he never owed anybody a cent, often paid bills with gold pieces.

Swart ordered that the safe be cracked, and he was disappointed to find only $1,640 in cash (enough money to buy two automobiles in 1919). If money were a motive for the murder, it could be ruled out now.

With the knowledge of the contents of the safe, Swart walked to Sarah Coburn's spartan bedroom at the back of the house. The drab shades were drawn, and Dr. Thompson had begun the autopsy. A survey of the room told Swart that there had not been a death struggle; not a piece of furniture was knocked over. Even the coal-oil lamp stood upright, and it was still lit. Sarah Coburn must have been in a deep sleep. Since the outside door that led into the back of the house was also unlocked, Swart deduced that the killer or killers could have entered by either the front or the back door.

The alleged weapon, the firewood club, was removed as evidence.

In the early hours of the investigation, Wally could not be ruled out as the prime suspect. Sheriff Sheehan tried to interrogate him, who, if he hadn't murdered his stepmother, could have witnessed the crime; maybe he could provide a clue, however small. It was a hopeless exercise. To all questions he mumbled: "I suppose". As a suspect, Wally was taken away for twenty-four-hour observation. Loren and Sarah never allowed the uncontrollable "boy" to ride in a horse and carriage, and certainly he never rode in the motor car they had purchased in 1910. He was permitted daily walks with Mrs. Joe Quilla, his hand firmly grasped by the strong Portuguese woman; but it was thought to be safer to keep him confined to the house. Now that his stepmother was dead, Wally took his first automobile ride over the mountains with the sheriff's guards. He was taken to Gardiner's Sanitarium, the former Belmont mansion of the wealthy banker William Ralston, builder of the vast Palace Hotel in San Francisco. The Sanitarium was a new world for Wally, who had known only the daily ritual in Pescadero.

The town divided regarding Wally's guilt. Carl Coburn, the "adopted son" of Loren, said that Wally could be the guilty party. In his opinion the boy had been behaving strangely and showing signs of violence. Neighbors claimed that they stopped the boy from trying to beat his stepmother, and that the day before the murder he was heard cursing and seen driving nails into a stick. Some people said that Wally grew violent when "crossed" and that perhaps Sarah had "crossed" him by failing to get up and help him when he asked her to.

Andy Stirling, a welcome guest who frequently visited Sarah, was most familiar with Wally's volcanic temper. He said he was there when Wally once swung a poker at Loren and Sarah. In his opinion Wally "...was very friendly toward Mrs. Harrison [the housekeeper] but seemed irritable toward Mrs. Coburn." Days before Sarah's murder Stirling saw Wally outside "driving nails into a plank". The noise aroused Sarah, and she came out to reprimand him. Stirling remembered her scolding: "Now, Wally, don't do that". Wally "cried and swore at her", and he began to "holler and then ran down the street..." On that occasion, as on many others, Wally had to be dragged back to the house.

Other Pescaderans said that Wally was the only other person in the house and obviously the killer. Besides—he scared people.

Wally's staunchest defenders pointed out that his mental condition prevented him from planning and carrying out a murder and that he was "the carefully selected camouflage of criminals better qualified to plot". Swart heard a report that two men drinking at the Elkhorn Saloon were seen tossing dice to determine which one of them would kill "Old Lady Coburn".

Mrs. Quilla, who knew Wally better than most people, did not believe he was capable of murder. But her husband, Joe, the ranchhand, disagreed: "...I used to be afraid of him," he volunteered. "...They said Wally would do anything." One time when Joe slept overnight in the Coburn house he secured the bedroom door with a rope, so that Wally could not barge in on him and scare him during the darkest hours of the night.

Meanwhile San Francisco Police Chief White, flanked by two detectives, had arrived by automobile. Accompanying them was Eustace Cullinan, one of Sarah Coburn's lawyers. Reporters and private detectives swarmed into the little village. Some were free-lance sleuths, hoping to cash in on the crime; others had been hired by relatives. Pescadero could not accommodate the streams of people pouring in; there were not enough rooms at the Swanton House to board the "hawkshaws".

A few detectives voiced their opinions at once: Wally could not have been the murderer, they said, because a light was necessary to accomplish the deed, and Wally was unable to light a coal-oil lamp. Swart delighted in snuffing out their theory: he said that Wally did not have to know how to light the coal-oil lamp because it was kept burning day and night.

Details of the Sarah Coburn murder story were splashed across the front pages of the San Francisco, San Mateo, and Monterey County newspapers. There was an accompanying photograph of the prim-looking former spinster—wearing a large beribboned hat beneath which was revealed an expressionless face with thin lips, almond-shaped eyes, and arched brows that looked penciled.

# THE LIVERY-STABLE BUSINESS

*"Mr. Coburn reminds me of one of those golden carps that live in Japanese ponds. He lies there with his mouth open and everything that comes to him he greedily absorbs; he gorges and he grows and grows until he is a big pondering mass of gold."*

—*Dr. J.W. Robertson, psychiatrist, 1909.*

On January 11, 1826, Loren Coburn was born into poverty, one of ten children, nine of them boys. The Coburns were religious folk who lived frugally in rural West Brookfield, Vermont, a community that lies in a "hanging valley" carved by glaciers. Soil on the hills surrounding West Brookfield is thin and stony; early settlers believed the stones that were forced to the surface by the seasonal freezing and thawing of the soil were the work of the devil.

The *Vermont Historical Gazeteer* proudly boasted that by 1871 West Brookfield had raised twenty-one ministers. Loren's parents, Clarinda Claflin and Ira Coburn, met during a religious revival in 1816. Clarinda, whose uncle was a minister, helped to organize the new Freewill Baptist Church which Ira joined. The couple married and had ten children: Ira Allen, Daniel Arza, Squire Alonzo, Loren, Julia Clarinda, Lemuel, Jesse Johnson, Jehiel Claflin, Silas Thomas Janison, and Henry Orris.

Then Clarinda died. Burdened with the boys, Ira searched for a new wife, and he found a widow named Mrs. John French. Perhaps it was Mrs. French, the mother of two children by her first marriage, who insisted that the Coburn boys be sent out on their own.

Loren must have found ways to earn money; his impoverished existence must have taught him to scrimp and save.

One popular story about Loren Coburn was told by Crittendon Thornton, a powerful San Francisco attorney with literary leanings. Thornton had litigated cases for Loren, and he presumed to know his client well. He said that when Loren was twelve and his parents had both died, he went to live with his older brothers in Massachusetts, where he was badly treated and then told to leave. This led Thornton to a theory: the rejection by his brothers caused Loren to seek revenge by dedicating his life to accumulating money.

The discovery of gold in California in 1849, when Coburn was twenty-three, must have given him an irresistible goal. He absorbed the tales of "striking it rich" in the Far West and was seduced by the promise of escaping poverty.

At last he got away. In April of 1851 Coburn boarded the U.S. Mail Steamship *Falcon*, choked with fortune hunters bound for Chagres, near the Isthmus of Panama. More than two years had elapsed since the discovery of gold, but the dream of unearthing a fortune in the new El Dorado beckoned him as strongly as it did the others.

Since Coburn was frugal, it is possible that he had heard of a bargain-rate passage from New York to San Francisco. For a short time competition for passengers helped the rates to drop to as low as one hundred dollars for a first-class cabin.

It was an arduous journey by sea, land, and jungle. Coburn crossed the Isthmus in a small boat, then rode a mule through the dense, green heat of the jungle and emerged at the Pacific Ocean.

There he and others boarded the steamer *Panama* and sailed up the Pacific coast to San Francisco. When he arrived in San Francisco on June 1, 1851, he was twenty-five years old.

He might have been disappointed by the barren headlands and treeless coastal hills; many passengers were. San Francisco was a place that had seen several disastrous fires. It was still a city of wooden houses, saloons, and sand hills. It was overcrowded and noisy, too, as men, horses, and wagons rumbled day and night through the streets of San Francisco.

Floating on the bay were fluttering "ghost ships" whose crews had taken off for the gold mines. California was an attraction for explorers, adventurers, and veterans of the Mexican War, all restless men looking for something to do. Average citizens carried derringers, toy-sized guns that were concealed on the body. When Coburn came in June of 1851, the first of the two famous Committees of Vigilance, consisting of wealthy, prominent San Franciscans, had been formed. The 184 men banded together with the goal of restoring law and order to their city.

Shadows obscure the first steps Loren took to begin pursuing his revenge, if we wish to believe attorney Crittendon Thornton's analysis. Most likely he headed for the gold fields, proceeding by river boat to Sacramento, then either on foot or by stagecoach to his destination. Newspaper biographies echo one another and say that Loren "mined for gold in the northern mines, where he remained for four months at the placers on the middle fork of the American River."

Mining probably suited Loren's secretive nature. Although it required extraordinary physical and mental strength, mining could be handled by only two men; one to dig the gravel, another to carry it and operate the rocker and sluice box.

Perhaps he was one of the lucky ones who came back to San Francisco with enough gold nuggets in a leather pouch to start a business. Or perhaps he bought a promising stake and sold it to another dreamer. He did return from the mines with enough capital to start a small business.

But which business did he start? Duncan McPherson, a *Santa Cruz Sentinel* reporter, who claimed to know Loren personally, wrote that "he prospered from the start" by setting up the first steam laundry in San Francisco. It is more commonly believed that Loren first owned a livery-stable in the village of Oakland. He commuted between Oakland and San Francisco on a near-empty ferry which dropped him off at the foot of Market street.

It is rumored that the profits from the Oakland stable were negligible and that after four years he put it up for sale. Coburn's critics, of whom there were many, charged that he went about this in an unethical manner.

Attorney Jubal Early Craig, who represented Loren and considered himself a friend of the family, confirmed that his client was "always a shrewd trader, always boosting the price of anything he is trying to sell and belittles anything he is trying to buy."

Profits from the Oakland sale enabled Loren to open a new stable in San Francisco, *The Horse Bazaar,* on Sansome Street between Washington and Jackson, which he ran as a place to board horses and as a carriage and auction house.

This area was the business and entertainment center of town. By 1860 banks, brokers' offices, public buildings, the leading hotels, retail stores, music halls, most of the lawyers, doctors, and saloons could be found there. The stable business gave him an opportunity to hear about land deals in the Bay Area. As an old man, Loren laughed as he recalled that he bought the stable "when most of San Francisco was a sandhill, and I could have bought most of the town for five thousand dollars."

As he achieved some financial success, Loren married Mary Antoinette Upton, a native of North Reading, Massachusetts. She was seven years his senior. Loren's new wife had two younger sisters: Sarah Satira and Anna Celestia, and a brother, Marraton. (A third sister, Laura, whose married name was Taylor, had died in San Francisco.) Later they would all live together in the tiny farming community of Pescadero.

The Uptons's father, Amos, was a mariner. In 1812 he sailed from Boston to Russia; he was with troops sent to invade France and overthrow Napoleon in 1815. Amos Upton further claimed to have met and talked with the powerful Emperor Napoleon in his rooms. This could explain the middle name of his daughter Mary.

In the early 1850's Mary Antoinette bore a son whom she named Wallace Loren. During their residence in San Francisco, the Coburns moved around. San Francisco directories show them residing at 1218 Jackson and at 2660 Jackson, but attorney Crittendon Thornton says he visited the family when they lived in a simple clapboard house at Capp and 24th Street, in today's Mission District.

Loren's livery-stable business did so well that he built a three-story brick building to house a new stable on the east side of Stockton Street near Washington.

Loren Coburn learned about land for sale near Pescadero, in San Mateo County, through Lloyd Tevis at the Hibernia Bank in San Francisco. Tevis, according to the *Santa Cruz Sentinel* reporter McPherson, had bought the Año Nuevo and Butano ranches, consisting of ten thousand five hundred acres, and the property of Captain Issac Graham, in a sheriff's sale. Coburn called on Tevis one morning in 1860 and asked if the ranches were for sale and for how much. Tevis quoted the price at twenty-four thousand dollars. With the help of Jeremiah Clark, a San Francisco land-grant attorney who bought half of the land, Coburn was able to secure the land within two hours.

But rumors persisted that Loren's riches had been accumulated dishonestly. There were stories that he stole from the elegant Spanish Dons who boarded their horses with him and were foolish enough to trust him to safeguard their elaborately hand-tooled leather saddles, embroidered with gold and silver. When the Dons returned, it was said that they were stunned to discover their priceless treasures replaced with cheap imitations. Loren denied any wrongdoing, and the Dons, whose foothold in California was tenuous, had no legal recourse. It was a time in history when the Americans were squatting on land once owned by the rancheros, and "rolling the Don" was a popular custom. This story, which has no basis in fact, followed Loren to his grave.

# THE PEBBLE BEACH AT PESCADERO

*The only road to Pebble Beach was "a kind of a zig zag...never laid out by anybody...[and it looked like] a cow trail because it was crooked, but wider because wagons crossed over it...The wind blows there like the blazes sometimes..."*

*—Alexander Moore, the pioneer farmer who built the first wood frame house in Pescadero about 1853.*

Some of the pebbles were as transparent as drops of dew, others were tinted rose, gold, or green. "Many are valuable gems," penned the editor of the *Coastside Advocate* in 1890, "such as carnelians, opals, cats-eyes, agates, moonstones, and water crystals, making it a profitable as well as a pleasant past time" to search the seashore.

Where did the shiny, colorful pebbles come from? Some people said they rolled into the Pacific Ocean from the cliffs. Others said it was the reverse: the tides swept the pebbles to the shore. But after the Gold Rush of 1849 and the Great Diamond Hoax of 1872, anything that sparkled on the ground might trigger a stampede. Pebble Beach was dubbed a "nautical wonder" and a "geologic freak".

The special beach was an attraction to new settlers and to tourists who braved the discomforts of the long, dusty stage ride over the mountains to the village of Pescadero.

It was two and a half miles from Mrs. Swanton's quaint hotel, along the winding cow-trail, past hills dotted with wild strawberries, to the famous Pebble Beach. The road took a sharp dip downwards toward the ocean, where the bluffs made access difficult.

The shoreline was rocky and the pebbles were ankle deep. Rolled and tumbled by the tides, the small stones were as smooth as silk. There seemed to be an endless variety of colors and shapes.

Yet this geological wonder, celebrated in Newton H. Chittenden's book, *Health and Pleasure Resorts of the Pacific Coast*, published in 1884, was only a quarter-mile in width and several hundred yards long.

Pebble Beach was enchanting. It became the proud centerpiece of Pescadero, "one of the most noted pleasure resorts on the entire coast".

"The first that I know of it being called Pebble Beach was in 1864," said the respected pioneer Alexander Moore. He heard "an old lady by the name of Hale who used to come down from a boarding house and a fellow by the name of Bill Carr" talk about the pebbles. "Ever since that time Pebble Beach has been a place of public resort."

Another story about its discovery by the outside world has been attributed to two San Francisco ladies, hunting for mosses, "when reaching this out-of-the-way spot after a scramble over the hills and rocks, we were astonished…to find a bed of gravel in which were mingled pebbles of the most beautiful hues and delicate shades of coloring." In this version Pebble Beach became famous overnight, and a steady stream of visitors appeared. The pebbles did not appear to diminish, although quantities of the stones were carried away. The local residents became enthusiastic pebble collectors. The prized pebbles were put on display or fashioned into rings, necklaces, and bracelets.

To reach Pebble Beach meant riding a horse or traveling in a buggy across a worn "road". Some chuck-holes had been filled in by stablemen who rented rigs to Pebble Beach visitors, but on the whole it was a poor excuse for a road.

For the villagers, Pebble Beach became the setting for their gatherings. J.C. Williamson, owner of the general store, who visited Pebble Beach a dozen times a year, remembered seeing three hundred picnickers there at one time. The Pescaderans held sumptuous picnics at Pebble Beach on many occasions. Pebble Beach became the strong element that held the community together.

Alexander Moore said that what took people there was "something good to eat at the picnics." He also said that with children, "We would go down there and lie on the pebbles." Unlike the others, this farmer did not go to sort through the pebbles. He confessed that he went because everybody else went to the beach, but in his lifetime he had never pocketed more than a dozen stones.

The prominent dairyman I.C. Steele went there "to take ladies and children and people to pick pebbles and play on the beach and picnic." The first time that Steele, who owned a large tract of land that he leased from Coburn south of Pescadero, saw Pebble Beach was in 1863 when he was riding horseback over the well-worn trail. From 1862 to 1872 Steele had seen "wagon loads, lumber wagons—there was scarcely anything else in the county there at the time"—traveling over the same well-worn path that the first pioneers had used to get to Pebble Beach. He suspected that if it weren't for the fascination of the pebbles, people would not have come back to the little beach again and again.

The condition of the "road" and how long the public had used it to get to Pebble Beach, would assume great importance in the 1890's.

Visitors needed a comfortable, friendly place to stay while they picked pebbles. Charles and Sarah Swanton offered accommodations in their row of six white cottages with false fronts, draped with trailing roses and climbing vines.

Each of the cozy cottages, separated by an alleyway, bore a name: Elm, Fern, Ivy, Myrtle, Rose, and Woodbine; in the rear they opened onto a common garden planted with colorful flowers and shrubs.

Charles and Sarah and their two children lived in the main house. Sarah, the former owner of a millinery shop, was an accomplished cook who nurtured a home-like environment at the Hotel.

An historic flagpole—a marker by which everyone measured distance—stood in front of the Swanton House. Although the flag vanished in later years, legend has it that it was made of store-bought blue flannel and sewn by the women in the village. Locals always mentioned the flagpole when giving directions to strangers.

Since the 1860's when the Swantons arrived in Pescadero from Maine, they had run this "plain country hotel with a good table". Charles never tired of showing off the natural wonders and curiosities of Pescadero. It was his affiliation with the Lighthouse Board that had brought him to northern California. Another reason the Swantons chose Pescadero as their home was that they owned stock in the U.S. Central Railroad. They believed that a railroad would be built from San Francisco south to Santa Cruz, a resort town on the Pacific Coast about thirty miles south of Pescadero. The Swantons could become rich.

In the 1870's Wooley and Taft's big stagecoaches picked up passengers daily at the San Mateo train station on the San Francisco Bay and carried them westward over the mountains to Pescadero. The uncomfortable stage ride took seven hours. With names like "Buckskin Bob", "Charlie", or "Ed", the stage drivers had reputations as hard drinkers and daring drivers who drove fast to please their anxious passengers. They showed off their skill on the crude, serpentine, mountain road and while snaking along the rugged coastline.

The drivers had occasional mishaps, such as the time that stage and passengers toppled into the Pacific Ocean. During a terrific wind storm one unfortunate stage driver was blown down a loading chute near Tunitas Creek and onto the deck of a moored steamer!

After leaving San Mateo, the passengers had views of the man-made Crystal Springs Lakes, which reminded one future landowner of Ireland. Then it was a precipitous climb up to the crest and a splash of whiskey at the Mountain House, before the driver plunged downward into the lush Pilarcitos Valley and the small farming community of Half Moon Bay.

On Main Street the horses got water and hay, and the driver tipped back another whiskey at the Index Saloon before racing along the last leg of the trip south to Pescadero. The stage weaved its way past thriving farms, dairies, and small settlements, until the spire of Pescadero's tiny white Congregational Church stood tall in the distance.

The wealthy traveled across the mountains in their own elegant four- and six-horse-drawn carriages. The Swanton House was a popular gathering place for the San Francisco railroad barons and the silver kings such as the Floods, the Crockers, and the McKays.

H.A. Schofield, the editor of the *San Mateo County Gazette*, described his trip to the Swanton House in glowing terms in June of 1871. He boarded the 8:50 a.m. train leaving Redwood City for San Mateo. At San Mateo Schofield took a seat in a "splendid" six-horse Concord coach and "pointed" for the Coast. He wrote: "...It was hard to find a more delightful and pleasant trip than it is at this season of the year to go from San Mateo to Pescadero. There is scarcely any dust to annoy the traveler, and the invigorating breeze constantly blowing from the broad Pacific renders it specially pleasant and comfortable after reaching the summit going to Halfmoon [sic] Bay...After eating a good dinner at the Dawson House in Halfmoon [sic] Bay the traveler is in good condition to enjoy the ride of eighteen miles down the coast to Pescadero—passing on the route the Purissima House and the San Gregorio House and arriving at Pescadero at half-past three o'clock p.m., where the smiling, good-natured,and accommodating Swanton is always on hand to give the guests of the Swanton House a cordial welcome."

The Swanton House buzzed with activity. Schofield checked the register and found that most of the hotel's guests were from northern California. He observed primarily women and children in the hotel, all of them excited about spending the afternoon at Pebble Beach. They were accommodated by a special stage that stopped at the hotel to pick up passengers for the short trip to the beach. Guests could also rent horses and carriages at any hour of the day from a former Santa Cruz County sheriff.

Sarah Swanton's official domain covered the parlors, billiard room, and kitchen. In the dining room she displayed a magnificent collection of pebbles and a cabinet full of marine and geological curiosities. Their daughter Eva, described as "a very agreeable aid", assisted her mother in making each visitor's stay pleasant. Business was so profitable that Charles's brother, Silas, came out west from Massachusetts. He bought a half interest in the Pescadero Livery Stable and lived in a house next door to the hotel. It was a house that Loren Coburn later bought.

One Santa Cruz writer described the breakfast Sarah prepared as consisting of mutton chops, beef steak, coffee, sweet milk, rich yellow butter, and mountain chickens. "After a sound night's sleep," she wrote, "the calm stillness of the morning is only broken by the singing of the birds, the echoes of the gurgling waters in the creek, or the roar of the surf on the beach."

In the afternoon Pebble Beach was the place to go. The women looked forward to finding dazzling stones that could be fashioned into necklaces or bracelets. "Those who have never seen or examined this wonderful, and I may say remarkable spot," raved 'Sigma' in the *Daily Alta Californian* in 1867, "can have but little conception of its character or the beautiful gems that lie scattered about on all sides, if one will only take the trouble to hunt for them…Here are found the carnelian, ruby, amethyst, emerald, garnet, amber and opal, the two latter being very pure and transparent…"

But what astonished 'Sigma' was the image of the pebble seekers: "…The costumes of pebble hunters are as varied as pebbles, while attitudes and positions are worthy of notice of an artist; from the cliff above, a full view of the scene may be had…Imagine a dozen females, some in bloomers and some without; some with long, some with short dresses, high boots and low-cut gaiters, straw hats, green veils, bandanas, and the inevitable shaker [believed to be a sunbonnet] lying about in every conceivable position, some on their knees and hands, others flat on their stomachs with hands busy, feet stretched out and hands half buried in holes they have made in the beach; others sitting, stooping, and in every position that suits them best. The scene is worthy the pencil of a painter, and if there were a wreck in sight, it would have the appearance of a number of bodies washed up by waves and left on the beach…"

"The most extraordinary part of it," marveled 'Sigma', "is that perfect silence is observed, and I only discovered the reason when on approaching a huge bundle of colored clothing surmounted by the antiquated shaker, unnatural and incoherent sounds emanating from under the shaker, and to my surprise discovered a well-known lady from

San Francisco (who wore her silks and fine bonnets there) who was so perfectly and admirably disguised that recognition was almost impossible…In an instant she took from her mouth a handful of pebbles which had been kept in that receptacle as a matter of convenience and pointing to me, exclaimed for the first time, 'beautiful, isn't it?'

"I now discovered the cause of this fearful silence among many females. They keep the pebbles in their mouths to test them and if satisfactory keep or throw them away."

Pebble Beach truly was a powerful attraction for a very brief moment in history.

The Swanton House was not the only hotel in town, but it was the most reputable and successful. In the earliest days, Postmaster Charles Kinsey and his wife Nancy ran a hotel, until they were arrested for the murder of a man named Harvey Green. There was also the windmill-powered Pescadero House and the Sulphur Springs Hotel, two miles east of the flagpole. But the cottages named Elm, Fern, Ivy, Myrtle, Rose, and Woodbine endured and outlived the competition.

For years Pebble Beach and the Swanton House provided fond memories of pleasant hours spent there. Too soon the villagers learned that Pebble Beach was located on land acquired by the controversial newcomer, Loren Coburn.

# THE LANDING AT PIGEON POINT

Horace Greeley, the famous editor of the *New York Tribune*, visited and wrote about California in the 1850's. Twenty years later a *Tribune* reporter, Colonel Albert S. Evans, came West for himself and wrote about his adventures in a book called *A La California, Sketches of Life in the Golden State*.

One of the towns Evans wandered into was tiny, isolated Pescadero, then ripe with optimism because someone was surveying and grading for a railroad from San Francisco to Pescadero.

What Colonel Evans saw was progress. Pescadero was no longer a village on two sides of a creek, but it now presented a "four-cornered front". The two-story attraction on San Gregorio Street was the McCormick Building, with a public hall and a suspended platform for musicians on the second floor. There were two blacksmith shops: Mr. Goulson repaired wagons, while Mr. Koster specialized in shoeing. There was a market, a harness shop, a barber shop, two livery stables, an express, telegraph, and post office. A new two-story, four-room public school was going up. Mrs. Hollingsead's private school was turning away applicants. The Library Association held its eighth anniversary meeting, and the members prided themselves on being the oldest library on the Coastside.

In addition to its reputation as a fine beach resort, Pescadero was a productive agricultural community. Grass covered the surrounding hills, and there were bountiful fields of potatoes, called "Irish oranges", and buckets of wild strawberries to pick.

No doubt Colonel Evans also heard about Loren Coburn, the man who owned some ten thousand acres surrounding Pescadero. There was talk that Coburn planned to build a boom at the mouth of Pescadero Creek to catch the stray logs floating down from the sawmills in the redwood forests. The hundreds of acres where vegetables were grown, where cows grazed and mammoth cheeses were produced, belonged to Loren Coburn.

Pigeon Point, six miles south of Pescadero and the only place with a suitable depth of water for a landing, was owned by Coburn. It was a highly desirable piece of property that Coburn had leased for ten years to investors, including a former San Mateo County Supervisor and a judge. They poured money into a new wharf, believing that shipping was a cheaper alternative for farmers and lumbermen than the railroad on the other side of the mountain.

Until then there had been a landing, but Coburn had not improved the old cable-rock arrangement; it took two and a half days' labor to load the steamers. The new investors modernized the wharf by extending the pier one hundred feet into the ocean. Shipping of local produce and lumber was dramatically improved; now a vessel could land alongside the wharf and load in four to six hours. The *Arcata* , a three-masted schooner, was one of the largest to stop there, and it stayed for one week. To further expedite the shipping of lumber to San Francisco, the investors planned to build a six-mile-long, three-foot-gauge railroad track from the redwood forests down to the landing. Those familiar with the old cable-rock loading technique wondered why Loren Coburn had not upgraded the wharf and reaped the rewards himself.

Another spur to development was the lighthouse built by the United States Government at Pigeon Point, at a cost of about ninety-five thousand dollars. Since 1853 when the *Carrier Pigeon* disappeared into a blanket of fog and crashed against the jagged rocks, there had been a public clamor for a lighthouse. Loren Coburn sold the land for it to the government.

The lighthouse stimulated the community called Pigeon Point Landing. There was a store and a school, and the blacksmith was building himself a house. Portuguese whalers and their families—some of whom later migrated the six miles north to Pescadero—lived in little cabins overlooking the picturesque semi-circular bay. A United States Post Office was established, and a member of the respected Steele family was appointed postmaster at Pigeon Point Landing.

The elegant lighthouse was a great source of pride for the Pescadero pioneers. Charles Swanton escorted hotel guests to view the lighthouse that was illuminated for the first time on November 15, 1872.

Swanton enjoyed talking about the lighthouse with its revolving fresnal light, manufactured in France. The lens mechanism operated with a weight hanging in the middle of the tower that had to be wound up like a grandfather clock. The source of light emanated from a series of wicks burning refined lard oil. (Until electricity reached Pigeon Point in the late 1920's, the light continued to work in this way.) The lens emitted white flashes every ten seconds, with eclipses in between. In clear weather it was visible from the deck of a vessel fifteen feet above the sea at a distance of eighteen and a half nautical miles.

The lighthouse measured twenty-seven feet at the base, and it had five-foot-thick walls. Some five hundred thousand bricks were used in the construction of the cone-shaped, white tower, whose dome was painted red. The railing, the brackets of the gallery, and other iron work at the top were painted black. The stairs, the platform, and the balcony were iron; the cylindrical structure had eight platforms diminishing in diameter as they ascended from fourteen to ten feet. Outbuildings stood north of the tower.

A steam whistle was installed south of Pigeon Point at Año Nuevo Island. It sounded blasts of fifteen seconds at intervals of forty-five seconds, and there was concern that this whistle could be confused with the signal at Pigeon Point.

A battle was brewing between the men who leased the landing at Pigeon Point and Loren Coburn, the landowner. The time was coming when the ten-year contract would expire, and they would have to relinquish the landing, but there were hints that they did not intend to do so.

# WALLY

*When Loren Coburn looked into his son's eyes and saw that reason and intelligence had fled, he vowed: "From this time on I shall lay on gold and then more gold."*

—*Crittendon Thornton, attorney.*

In 1866 Loren Coburn was forty and a very rich man. The money enabled Loren, his wife Mary Antoinette, and their young son Wallace to take a trip to the East Coast. Whether they traveled overland or by sea is unknown, as is where they lived, but the Coburns stayed for two years. Loren did visit the home of his older brother, Lemuel, a successful businessman living in Holyoke, Massachusetts. On that occasion, the Coburns met Lemuel's son, Arzo. The boy was close to Wally's age, and the two children played together.

After returning to San Francisco in 1868, Loren purchased more land —fifteen hundred acres in Merced County and some building lots in Fresno.

Already the largest landowner in San Mateo County, Loren Coburn picked up another ten thousand acres near King City in Monterey County. He lobbied the representatives of the powerful Southern Pacific Railroad—also known as "the Octopus"—in the hope that they would lay track through his land and build a train station there. He knew they were building a line from San Francisco to Monterey, where their centerpiece, the Del Monte Hotel, welcomed tourists to what was acclaimed as "the queen of American watering places". Coburn felt so optimistic about his chances of winning a train station that he christened his land Coburn.

Many years later during his visits to King City, he would make the acquaintance of J.A. Bardin, a major landowner and prominent descendent of pioneers, and Chris Widemann, a "land developer" and bon vivant.

It was during this prosperous period that seventeen-year-old Wally fell seriously ill and nearly died from what Loren called a severe case of "spotted fever". It might have been typhoid fever, as the newspapers reported, possibly brought on by poor sanitation, tainted water, or contaminated milk. The fever caused a delirious state of mind, and if he spoke, his speech was slurred, an omen of what was to come.

Wally lived, but as Loren later explained, when the fever left, his son's "mind was gone". The change in Wally was overwhelming. How the Coburns coped with this tragedy is part of the story. Although Loren lacked the education and poise, he had the financial means to lead an active social life if he chose. Now that possibility was closed forever.

A tall, good looking boy, Wally now required help with dressing and eating. A leather apron would be draped around him before he sat down at the kitchen table. He got fresh air on tightly supervised walks, with someone leading him and gripping his hand. He could not be left alone; it was best to keep Wally in the house.

Wally did display an unusual talent for playing the piano. The Coburns had a piano delivered to California in a ship that sailed around the Horn. Wally loved to play the instrument, and he would repeatedly ask: "Can I see my piano? Can I play my piano?"

He was called "the boy", a nickname which best describes his new mental state.

Sarah Satira Upton, his mother's younger sister, knew Wally before and after his tragic bout with "spotted fever". In 1873 when she was a plain-looking thirty-five-year-old spinster, Sarah left her father's house in Vermont and visited the Loren Coburns in San Francisco. She was an excellent housekeeper. Loren put her to work; she was paid twenty-five dollars a month to do the housekeeping. Wally was about sixteen, and Sarah said that his "mental condition was nice and bright. He was then all right and was going to school."

After a year she returned to Vermont. Two years later when Sarah came back to San Francisco she said that Wally "...had his sickness in the meantime, and he has been an imbecile ever since." Besides housekeeping, her duties now included looking after the "mentally weak" boy. Loren admired her loyalty and gentleness with his son.

Wally's illness affected his mother's health. She frequently complained of ailments and became so ill that she begged her younger sister Sarah to promise to look after Wally if she should die. Sarah promised.

Apparently Loren never considered an institution as an option for "the boy", which led cynics to accuse him of being too cheap to help his son.

To that Loren responded: "There is only one place for Wally and that is home. He is my son, and he shall stay here and have everything he wants so long as he lives." Loren said he would give up most of his wealth in return for his son's mental health. But that pact could not be tested.

His son's irreversible mental condition soured Loren's already testy disposition. Embittered, he lashed out at others.

Pescadero was rife with suspicions and rumors regarding how Loren accumulated his wealth and his land. This was compounded when he refused to pay a special tax for a new schoolhouse and went to the extreme measure of filling out an official protest form. He won on a technicality; but he lost the friendship of his neighbors. From that time forward the newspapers frequently portrayed him as a big, rich landowner who would not help the community.

After Wally's illness, the Coburns moved from San Francisco to their dairy on the fourteen hundred acre ranch near Pigeon Point. The family could have remained in San Francisco, said Loren, but "Wally would be the object of public gaze there... Wally is happy and contented where he is. If I moved [back] to San Francisco, people wouldn't understand like the people in Pescadero, and he wouldn't be happy."

Many Pescaderans were convinced that Wally was born mentally retarded.

At Pigeon Point Loren hired a Chinese servant named Ah Gee to watch over his son. One of his duties was to feed "the boy" at the dining room table.

"Ah Gee is kind to Wally," said Sarah. "When he goes to take a nap, Gee will go and look at him, put his fingers on his temples, feel his pulse, and feel his heart and see that everything is alright."

# A SHOOT-OUT AT PIGEON POINT

*"The people of Pescadero were with the steamship company."*
—Duncan McPherson, Santa Cruz Sentinel, *1891.*

Pigeon Point Landing "...attracted the attention of an unscrupulous ring of speculators, composed of officials and ex-officials of San Mateo County," wrote San Francisco attorney Crittendon Thornton. "They determined to get hold of the property by hook or by crook and to use it for their own purposes."

The speculators included the poker-playing Judge Horace Templeton, the pipe-smoking former Supervisor Josiah P. Ames, who had been described as a "bold, bad man", and Charles Goodall, the head of the Pacific Coast Steamship Company. Judge Templeton had interests in the sawmill business in the nearby Gazos Creek area. Ames was the force behind busy little Amesport Landing, four miles north of Half Moon Bay, where a colorful community sprang up around the wharf. Goodall's steamers picked up the local produce there.

The move to Pigeon Point may have been part of Loren's strategy. It gave him an excellent opportunity to watch over activities at the busy landing. The ten-year lease was about to expire in 1872, and he was anxious to take over the successful wharf operation.

Would these men give up the profitable Pigeon Point Landing in 1872?

Before the lease ran out, the men had considered protecting their investment by running a railroad across Loren's land, which would give them outside access to the wharf. So they incorporated the Pigeon Point Railroad and brought in a new investor, the mining millionaire George Hearst.

The lease with Coburn expired, but the men had no intention of honoring the contract. When Loren told Ames, Templeton, and Goodall to vacate Pigeon Point Landing, they offered to buy the land, but Loren refused to sell. Then they refused to leave. By summer Coburn tried to evict the men unsuccessfully. The Pescaderans, who opposed Loren because he had refused to pay the school tax, sided with the speculators. The villagers were not impressed with this "San Francisco Capitalist" who wore black swallow-tail coats, talked too fast, and drove his horses recklessly across the countryside.

Using their political connections, Ames and Templeton petitioned the Board of Supervisors for a wharf franchise, proposing to further modernize the facilities in return for twenty years of use. The petition failed, but the County responded favorably by condemning the land and surveying a road which ran to the end of the loading chute.

Coburn retaliated by sending his lawyer to the State District Court in San Francisco. The court reversed the condemnation on the grounds that the lands were not properly identified and that the road to the wharf was a private road. *The only public property, said the court, was the land within high tide.*

Despite the ruling, Loren could not get physical possession of the landing. The sheriff who accompanied him with the court order claimed that he was not certain from the document where the property was located.

Into the battle walked C.N. Fox, a former county attorney, now employed by Judge Templeton. Fox appealed to the State Supreme Court on behalf of his clients. Complaints, court orders, counter orders, and injunctions criss-crossed desks for twelve months.

Most of the wharf extended into the high tide, and the shrewd investors saw that it was to their advantage to separate it from the private land. The men put up a gate across the wharf at the point where it stretched one hundred feet into the high tide, thus officially disconnecting the public property where they conducted business from Coburn's private property. Armed with a navy six-shooter, Alexander "Scotty" Rae was hired to watch over the sanctity of the gate.

Although the lease had expired, and the San Francisco court ruled that Loren should have his land back, the shipping operation continued.

While visiting Pigeon Point Landing in February of 1873, Judge Templeton fell down a cliff, struck his head, and was seriously injured. Was he pushed by one of Coburn's men as a warning of the violence to come? The judge fell ill and died of other causes in December of the same year. The investors continued working on the high-tide side of the wharf.

When the State Supreme Court finally awarded Coburn possession of the wharf, Ames and Goodall still would not move. Coburn's lawyer, San Francisco attorney William Craig, advised him to take possession of the wharf peacefully. He assured his client that the law would protect him. But this time Loren hired four gun-fighters in San Francisco and brought them back to Pigeon Point.

During a night in July of 1875 the gunslingers took possession of the loading chute and built a breastwork of planks two feet high across the chute. In the early morning hours when Scotty, who shared an office with the telegraph operator, saw the fortifications, he reached for his navy six-shooter. He rushed down the chute, cursing and threatening as he advanced—this despite the number of cocked guns pointed at him. The gun fighters warned Scotty that he had better not set foot on the wharf. The argument heated up, and Scotty impulsively fired at one of the men and missed. In the flash of a gun he was a corpse; five balls were lodged in his body, one through the heart.

Several Portuguese whalers witnessed the shooting, but they did not interfere.

When news of Scotty's murder reached Pescadero, the sentiment against Loren was intense. "Lynch him, lynch him," was the cry as a mob stormed Pigeon Point.

A few hours after Scotty's murder, the County Coroner impanelled a jury of Pescaderans for the inquest. After quick deliberation, Loren and the four hired gunfighters were charged with murder. At the Redwood City jail, Loren was released on a ten-thousand-dollar bond.

Five days later a hearing was held in Redwood City. Coburn's lawyer produced the Portuguese whalers as witnesses. They testified that three of the gunfighters were at the end of the wharf behind a low gate when Scotty approached them. The gunfighter named Wolfe seemed to be in charge. He did the talking and held up his open right hand. Scotty advanced to the fence and tried to push it down, but failed. He stepped back and shot twice at Wolfe, who bowed respectfully in recognition of each charge. Then several shots were fired and Scotty fell.

The whalers said Coburn was at the land end of the chute when Scotty was killed.

Coburn and his hired guns posted bail. Two trials followed; the first one in February, 1876, was delayed because the defendants refused to be tried together; jury selection also proved to be difficult. Wolfe pleaded self-defense. Conflicting testimony resulted in a hung jury.

The second trial began three months later. Judge Daingerfield told the jury that the evidence was insufficient for a conviction and that the verdict of not guilty was mandatory. The Pescaderans now had proof that Loren Coburn thought he was above the law. In later years questions arose as to whether Loren regularly bribed judges and juries. It was not an uncommon practice.

More significantly, Judge Daingerfield made a "final" decision regarding Pigeon Point. He awarded the wharf, chute, and roads to Loren Coburn.

Feeling vindicated, Loren rode to Pigeon Point with the San Mateo County Sheriff to enforce the Judge's legal order to vacate. But while they were riding over the mountains, the decision was appealed! Incredibly, Coburn was once again blocked from taking back his land.

For two days Coburn watched freight flow steadily across his private property, with all the proceeds going to someone else. On the third day, he shoved his wooden office shed to a spot where it obstructed the movement of commerce. Upon hearing this, Judge Daingerfield ordered him to remove the shed. The wharf's employees, who hated Coburn, tossed the shed onto the rocks below.

Finally, in 1878, six years after the trouble started, after the murder of "Scotty" Rae, and after endless amounts of cash had been poured into litigation, the California Supreme Court awarded the landing to Coburn. By this time, lack of interest and the expensive legal fight had drained the reserves of his opponents. Southern Pacific Railroad officials were negotiating with shippers such as the Pacific Mail steamship company to fix freight costs and thereby suppress competition. There were rumors that both parties squandered twice the value of the property. But Loren Coburn now had control over the loading chute and the warehouse at Pigeon Point. He finally had possession of the land which belonged to him.

# THE COBURN CLAN ARRIVES

After living for a time at the Pigeon Point Ranch the Coburns moved to Pescadero, to an eight-room house on San Gregorio Street. An emblem of a rising sun was visible on an exterior gable facing the street. Loren Coburn bought the story-and-a-half cottage from Charles Swanton's brother. The general store, the Elkhorn Saloon, and other businesses stood on this street. Falling back on his former trade, Loren opened a livery stable; the large checkerboard shingle hanging in front identified it as the Eureka Stable.

He also continued to buy land, this time the Gazos Mill property, once owned by his enemy, Judge Templeton. The Gazos property included the mill, buildings, and timber, but it had had a trail of bad luck. Hundreds of Chinese were employed at the Mill, grading and timber-cutting for railroad ties. The wood was shipped from Pigeon Point to San Francisco. There were grandiose plans to run the mills day and night to turn out fifty thousand feet of shingles, lumber, and ties, but the chute could not handle the volume and nothing came of it.

The Chinese, driven out of San Francisco by labor laws against them, opened Chinese laundries and were welcomed by Pescaderans, but within a few years they were all gone, except for Loren's servant, Ah Gee.

Loren frequently traveled south to King City to inspect the ten-thousand-acre ranch he owned there. On his return one day, he found that his brother, JC, and wife, Lucy, and ten-year-old adopted son Carl had arrived from Vermont, to live with them for six months. The family returned to Vermont, but came back to Pescadero a year later. In an act of unprecedented generosity toward his brother and with a gesture of interest in his nephew Carl, Loren bought a building lot for the Coburn family, three hundred feet away from his own house. "I gave him a place there," Loren later explained about the JC Coburn house. "I made a present to him."

JC, a carpenter and a machinist, who was "universally respected", and his wife, Lucy, who occasionally conducted evening services at the white clapboard Congregational Church down the street, built a house where they set up a bakery. They took in overnight guests for additional income. Jobs were scarce.

Loren Coburn liked his young nephew Carl Coburn, a clever boy with wavy hair and ears that stuck out, seeing in him the son he would never have, the young man his demented son Wally might have been. Given a good education, Carl grew up watching his Uncle Loren, observing his business dealings, and charming the local citizens with his eagerness. He learned that Loren's hallmark was never to sell any of his land.

He also observed the beginnings of a battle stirring between his Uncle Loren and the Pescaderans. To protect his private property from trespassers, Loren was putting up fences as early as 1874 and closing private roads located on his land, roads that had previously been freely used by the public. One of the roads that he closed led from Pescadero to Pigeon Point; the County had to pay him an exorbitant fee for this right-of-way. It was almost a matter of common courtesy to allow people to cross over private land, but Loren balked at the idea. He was not a friendly man.

Aunt Sarah Upton, the sister of Mary Antoinette, whose health was failing, had moved into Loren's house and cultivated a "calling acquaintance" with the JC Coburns. As a housekeeper and companion to Wally, she had been the most welcome of a steady stream of the Coburn's relatives who began to appear at the rich man's doorstep. Unlike the others, she was not poor; Sarah had apparently inherited fifty thousand dollars worth of property from her father.

Least welcome was Marraton Upton, Sarah and Mary Antoinette's brother, then in his sixties and a homeless widower with a scraggly white beard stained with tobacco juice. He was quickly named "Whiskers" by the children, who teased him relentlessly.

Marraton thought of himself as an "old Indian fighter", but he wore long, black frock coats, a broad-brimmed black hat, and he shuffled when he walked. He had a serious drinking problem. When he was not drowning in twenty-five-cent bottles of whiskey at one of the several saloons, he was sleeping off hangovers in the Coburn house.

"Whiskers" embarrassed Loren, who did not smoke or drink. He put Marraton to work at the Eureka Stable keeping the books; that was an unwise decision.

Along with Ah Gee, the Chinese servant, Marraton was also assigned to keep an eye on Wally. But he was drunk most of the time and could not be relied upon. When Marraton drank he talked too much. The boys in town gladly plied him with whiskey, because as Coburn's bookkeeper, he would forgive their debts when he was drunk.

Sarah and Marraton's other sister, Anna Celestia, a spinster in her fifties, was the next to arrive from the East Coast, and she immediately fell ill. Anna Celestia—who took an intense dislike to Loren—was bedridden most of the time. How much she despised her brother-in-law became clear as she periodically tried to terrify the sixty-six-year-old man into turning over his property to her by waving in his face a blank commitment to Agnews Insane Asylum.

Harmony could not be bought at any price. Living under one unhappy roof were Loren, his wife Mary Antoinette, who was now dying of cancer; Wally, their mentally ill son; Ah Gee, the Chinese servant; Sarah, the loyal housekeeper; Anna Celestia, the disagreeable sister-in-law; and Marraton the drunkard.

The family met for meals in the small, dreary dining room dominated by a large safe filled with cash and gold.

Lemuel Coburn, a well-to-do businessman from Massachusetts, created a welcome diversion when he came to visit his brother. His company manufactured door hangers for sliding doors, and he was eyeing the trolley-car market.

"The hangers are far ahead of any yet seen here and will be used on outside doors," enthused the Pescadero correspondent for a San Mateo County newspaper. Lemuel's son, Arzo, the childhood playmate of Wally, was now a grown man, and he came with his wife. He struck up an immediate friendship with Carl, whom he could see shared the complete confidence of Uncle Loren.

Yet another brother, Alonzo, a seriously ill widower, came to live out his days in Pescadero. He moved in with J.C.'s family across the street. But the fact that Alonzo lived under a different roof made little difference to Loren.

His life had become what he called "a perfect hell".

# BAD TIMES

*"This whole matter was got up by a few speculators, seeking pebbles to sell…"*

—*Loren Coburn, 1891.*


In 1885 a strong southeast wind destroyed Loren's loading chute and warehouse at Pigeon Point. The chute was rebuilt by a shingle-mill owner whose own mill had been destroyed twice by burning sawdust piles.

Despite the reassuring presence of the Pigeon Point Lighthouse, the barque *J.W. Seavey* went ashore; her waterlogged sailors passed through the village.

The forty-thousand-dollar Sulphur Springs Hotel burned to the ground and was not going to be rebuilt. The Pescadero House was sold. The avuncular Charles Swanton was declared insane and confined to a sanitarium in Napa where he died at age fifty-eight. Sarah Swanton carried on alone and was still running the well-known hotel in 1889.

Finally, the railroad disappointed the people. Alvinza Hayward ran out of cash during the early construction. A man called Colonel Bridges turned out to be ineffectual; money and time invested in surveys and maps produced nothing. Pescadero remained isolated.

A new scheme called for a "bicycle railroad" to run from Millbrae on the San Francisco Bay over the mountains to Pescadero. A "decided novelty", the bicycle railroad would be an economy railroad system that consisted of a single rail and a single set of wheels under the cars. Like a bicycle, it was self-supporting. Construction costs would be minimal, because the road could be built over grades and through country where a narrow-gauge could not hope to follow. And it would reach speeds up to one hundred miles-per-hour without causing passengers any discomfort.

When that scheme failed, there seemed to be better news: the West Shore Railroad Company proposed to operate between San Francisco and Santa Cruz. It was learned that Loren Coburn had made a secret agreement with the railroad: what the West Shore received in return we cannot know for certain, but it was probably land or rights-of-way. Work was to begin in 1897. Loren demanded that two stations be built at Pebble Beach; one of them would be named Coburnville.

The Pescaderans were stunned when they heard that Loren was going to build a two-story hotel and a townsite at Pebble Beach. But they were appalled when he forbid the public to visit Pebble Beach at all. He gave notice that "the carrying away of colored stones would be regarded as highway robbery". Trespassers had reason to fear Coburn; his hired gunfighters had killed Scotty Rae over the possession of Pigeon Point Landing.

Since the leisurely days of the rancheros, it had been a custom to allow travelers to cross over privately-owned land. The villagers had always used the roads on private property, until Loren Coburn turned mean. In 1880 he tacked up one of his first signs, announcing that he was closing a main road on his property, citing the unsafe condition of bridges in the area. The road-closing inconvenienced the villagers and should have served as a warning of what was to come. The notice did not bother to state when or, if, the road would ever reopen.

The Pebble Beach Road, a crooked trail worn by wagon wheels, horses, and humans, that led from Pescadero to Pebble Beach, was closed in September of 1891. The gate had not been closed before.

Loren "claims Pebble Beach and all its pebbles," fumed the *San Mateo Times & Gazette*. "The people are a unit in expressing their indignation at this move on the part of Mr. Coburn; even the schoolchildren are in open rebellion at the usurpation of what they consider their lawful… playground."

Another newspaper huffed: "L. Coburn, who owns the land lying between the county road and the ocean, has locked the gate on the road leading to the beach which has been open to the public for thirty years, and he emphatically forbids trespassing on his property. As there is no other access to the beach, the action appears a piece of spiteful officiousness. What Mr. Coburn's motive is we cannot conceive, as the road through his land does not injure it in any way, and, as he is one of the largest landowners in this section, it seems that he would be vitally interested in the progress and popularity of Pescadero, instead of depriving it of its chief attraction..."

Coburn defended his locking of the gate: He had rented the land to farmers James Wilson and John Montevaldo, but both men had declined to renew their leases because the traffic to and from Pebble Beach annoyed them.

"...Wilson...told me," said Loren, " 'I can't pay you rent for this ranch. They come and leave the gates open, and they go through here and trespass on me. I can't keep the people off.' " Loren's advice to Wilson was to lock the gates, but the farmer replied " 'If I lock the gates they break them down.' "

"You had better lock the gates," warned Loren, "because you have got it under lease." Wilson refused, but he asked for a reduction in the rent, and when it was not forthcoming, he moved away. Montevaldo, apparently, did try locking the gates, but he, too, wanted to renegotiate the lease.

Loren complained that the trespassers came in "mobs" of sixty or seventy and that they staked out forty horses at a time and picked the wild strawberries. Allegedly, Loren said anyone who did not trample the strawberries could visit Pebble Beach. All they had to do was ask him for the key.

But it wasn't quite that simple. According to Alex Moore, Loren said that strangers would be carried to the beach, from his stable, of course, for seventy-five cents per head. Mr. Moore then inquired, "What about our women and children?", to which Loren replied spitefully, "They have no business here."

Many Pescaderans questioned Loren's legal right to Pebble Beach; they said "the Czar" had made himself "universally unpopular by this action".

If it was a well-worn road used for thirty or more years, they asked, didn't it qualify as a public road? Since it had been used as a highway for more than five years, the road could not be closed to the public without special action by the Board of Supervisors. From their perspective, the people had a right to reach the beach that lay below the high water mark because it was government tideland.

This group petitioned the Supervisors and asked them to condemn a road across Loren's property, in order to reach the beach "which is supposed to be neutral or government ground". The outcome, it was believed, could have an impact on citizens throughout the country.

Loren and the Pescaderans clashed on the length of time the Pebble Beach Road had been used by the public. Loren said when he first bought the ranch nobody knew much about Pebble Beach. It was later that the farm became famous "from Shasta to Tia Juana as a producer of precious stones".

Visitors, said Loren, could "get from most anywhere to Pebble Beach without any roads. You can drive a buggy without any road from most anywhere." Loren added that the trail was four or five inches deep and that the wagons have "run a little while in one track and then they would take another track…" He did not acknowledge the existence of the so-called Pebble Beach Road.

# THE LEVY BROS

The arrival of the enterprising Levy brothers injected new energy into the community. Joe Levy was appointed postmaster in 1885. His brothers Armand, the piccolo player in the Pescadero Cornet Band, and Ferdinand helped run the stage business and the successful chain of general stores.

The Levy brothers opened the store in the old McCormick Building, the former "attraction on the road", near the Swanton House and around the corner from the Elkhorn saloon. Besides dry goods and groceries, there was a drug store, Wells Fargo agency, Western Union, and U.S. Post Office within the general store.

The well-liked J.C. Williamson, then about thirty years old, was hired to juggle the roles of druggist, telegraph operator, and clerk. He was also the Pescadero correspondent for the *San Mateo Times & Gazette.* Williamson learned the general-store trade so thoroughly that he opened his own business across from Loren Coburn's house. For thirty-five years, Williamson's store served as the village bank, lending money at no interest. Williamson succeeded Joe Levy as postmaster.

The productive Levys built a new stable and started up a rival stage-line running between Pescadero and San Mateo. They bought a timber tract on Butano Creek and built a shingle mill.

Of the three brothers, Joe was the most confrontational. He was bound to conflict with Loren, the largest landowner. The brothers became acquainted with Loren when they rented his land near Pigeon Point Landing for a big dairy operation, where they installed the latest steam-powered cheese equipment.

Now in his late sixties, Loren was derisively called "Mr. Moneybags" and "The Judge", because of the ease with which he settled his legal problems outside of the courtroom.

# THE FIRST CONFRONTATION – 1891

The locked gate fired up Joe Levy's sensibilities, and he announced a "Grand Picnic" at Pebble Beach on Saturday, September 12, 1891. Some fifty disgruntled Pescaderans answered his call for a protest and climbed into a caravan of private coaches and wagons. Besides Levy, the ringleaders included San Mateo County Supervisor Henry B. Adair and Roadmaster Charles R. Pinkham, a former fast-freight operator. The triumvirate intended to storm the gate.

The man sitting in the rear seat of the lead Concord Coach, drawn by four horses, steadied an effigy that bore a close resemblance to Loren. Five two-horse buggies, five singles, and several one-horse wagons lined up to navigate the squiggily road to Pebble Beach.

At the same time sixty-one-year-old Sarah Upton was riding with her brother Marraton from Pigeon Point to Pescadero. When she ran into "the mob" at 1 p.m. her mood was testy.

"…I said to my brother, 'They are going to break down that gate.' I had hardly got the words out of my mouth when they did…" She saw the effigy and heard the passengers refer to it as Loren, but Sarah saw no physical resemblance.

Pinkham, the bold roadmaster, and his assistants marched to the gate. It was strongly barricaded: Two heavy twelve-inch piles had been sunk deep into the ground. Across them two heavy pine two-by-twelve bridge planks had been fastened with eight-inch iron spikes. Two heavy cable chains with padlocks secured the ends of the gate.

Pinkham removed the obstructions.

"…They took a board of some kind," recalled Sarah, "and went to the lock on the gate and broke through, and then they shouted and went down to the beach."

"Certainly," agreed J.C. Williamson, "that is the only way we had of getting through there." Williamson, who was one of the protesters, said the gate "…was barred up, planked up across from one post to another and spiked together." He didn't see any "Keep Out" signs. He came for one reason only; he thought it was wrong of Loren to lock the gate.

The wild and belligerent behavior of the men seemed out of place. "…they hollered and swore…,"said Sarah. She heard them boast as they swung the effigy that "they would lay old Coburn in the dust…"

Loren was not there that day, but some witnesses said they saw the mob burn his effigy. Joe Levy denied it. "…That Mr. Coburn was burnt in effigy," refuted another citizen, "stands branded as another lie, as the effigy is still in prime condition and will be preserved."

Once the gate had been trampled, the men became civilized, and "a more orderly, quiet, or harmonious assemblage never met on the beach… This case of a united people without a dissenting voice, pitted against a grasping, miserly, avaricious money-bags stands without parallel."

Supervisor Henry B. Adair, who had held the job of roadmaster before Pinkham, was accused of acting on behalf of the County Board of Supervisors. He vigorously denied it. "I was told the gate was locked, and I went and saw for myself that it was…," maintained Adair.

The next day, Sunday, "Boss Coburn" dispatched his men to re-barricade the gate. Coburn ordered Pinkham, who was on the scene, "to let that gate alone", but the roadmaster turned a deaf ear and promptly removed the obstructions again.

First thing Monday morning Loren rode to the county seat at Redwood City and had a warrant issued for the arrest of Joe Levy, charging him with breaking down Coburn's fence, a misdemeanor. Levy received news of the warrant in a telegram sent to the Western Union office in his general store. He rode to Redwood City and asked Justice Welch for time before pleading. Levy was released on his own recognizance.

A jury was selected for "the People versus Levy", better known as "that Pescadero case". San Francisco attorney Crittendon Thornton represented Loren. Levy defended his actions by saying he broke down the gate because Coburn had illegally obstructed a public road that had been used for thirty years. Joe Levy was acquitted.

A month later Pebble Beach was open to all, and several "mammoth" picnics were planned. Pebble hunters came and went without incident.

The confrontation with Joe Levy did not end at the Pebble Beach gate. It was to expand into a business rivalry. The following spring Loren jumped into the stage business and bought two, roomy, Mt. Hamilton coaches, each capable of holding eleven passengers. Called the People's Stage Line, it covered the San Mateo-Half Moon Bay-Pescadero route.

Was it coincidence that Joe Levy also owned a stage line that covered the same territory?

Fares would be low on the People's Stage Line, vowed Loren, much lower than the competition. In May Coburn charged one and a half dollars from Pescadero to San Mateo in "fine coaches with careful drivers". In June passengers paid ninety-five cents to travel from Pescadero to San Francisco. Joe Levy matched the low fares, and most travelers chose to board his coaches; thus the fare war ended.

Coburn had ordered more coaches; he wanted to run three daily stages, but a glitch at Half Moon Bay, where Levy Bros. had their flagship general store, put a halt to his ambitious plans.

# PART II

## THE WEALTHY LANDOWNER

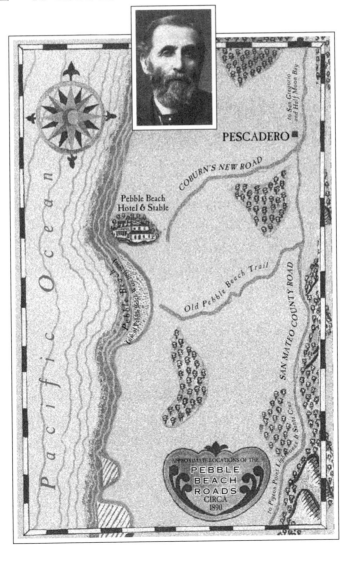

Pacific Ocean

PESCADERO

COBURN'S NEW ROAD

Pebble Beach Hotel & Stable

Old Pebble Beach Trail

SAN MATEO COUNTY ROAD

to San Gregorio and Half Moon Bay

to Pigeon Point Lighthouse & Santa Cruz

APPROXIMATE LOCATIONS OF THE
PEBBLE BEACH ROADS
CIRCA 1890

# CHAPTER ELEVEN

# PRIVATE PROPERTY OR PUBLIC?

If Loren Coburn could not stop the Pescaderans from riding over their beloved cow trail, he would build a new, level road from Pescadero to the mouth of Pescadero Creek, along the shore to Pebble Beach, then south to connect with the County road at Bean Hollow. It would cost eighteen hundred dollars.

Did this new road show a benevolent side of Loren?

"Coburn pays the bills and doesn't look as if he wanted to close Pebble Beach to the public," granted former critics.

Then Coburn disappointed them by locking the gate to Pebble Beach. The gate was torn down, rebuilt, torn down, rebuilt...Supervisor Adair described the damage: "...These planks [that had been] spiked across had been nailed and pried open and nailed and pried open until in fact there was nothing of the gate left..."

A bruising editorial charged: "...Coburn claims the beach itself, and tells people who take pebbles from it they are committing grand larceny. As the beach is covered every day with ocean tides, his claims are preposterous..."

Was his plan to close the old Pebble Beach road, the cow trail, and charge a fee for using his new road?

The new Pebble Beach road was suspect, because it had not been "dedicated to the public, and the people will not use it since they believe it is a subterfuge to get them to abandon the old road, whereupon they would lose both." The editorial recommended that "the state should buy or condemn a roadway to this beach and keep it open to the public. Then when the public has unrestricted access, someone under proper restriction should be allowed to build a casino on the shore, and in one summer Pebble Beach would rise in popularity as a resort second to none on the coast..."

The man with a solution was Assemblyman James T. O'Keefe, a promising young attorney who acknowledged that Pebble Beach was a great tourist resort. He introduced Assembly Bill #103, which would dedicate Pebble Beach to San Mateo County as a public park. Senator Bart Burke of Santa Cruz shepherded the bill through the state legislature in Sacramento.

"The passage of the bill will forever set to rest any controversy as to the present ownership and right of way," penned the Pescadero correspondent J.C. Williamson.

Loren's reaction to the proposed legislation was, "They are trying to steal my land." He pointed to his Mexican land grant which he claimed guaranteed him his property rights.

In February, 1893, Assembly Bill #103 passed both houses unanimously, giving San Mateo County legal guardianship over the beach of pebbles.

But there was a loophole: the bill failed to provide for a road or a right-of-way from the public highway across Loren's private land to the beach. Even so, the Pescaderans felt they had won the "war". There were demands that the County immediately open a road to the beach.

Passage of the bill led to rejoicing. A seashore banquet to celebrate "Pescadero's inheritance" was announced, and an invitation extended to all the neighboring towns. The State Legislators Burke and O'Keefe were special guests. Flags flapped in the breeze over every roof-top, and businesses closed their doors for the day.

Crunching his leather soles on the pebbles was Dr. McCracken, Pescadero's spokesman and a future County Supervisor. "Ladies and Gentlemen," he greeted the fifteen hundred well-wishers, "... For over a year the people have been battling for their rights..."

Senator Burke ingratiated himself: "...looking into the faces of the good people present and feeling as I now do the motives which have actuated you to battle for the freedom of these grounds and above all being an eye witness to the happiness and pleasure it gives the entire community to feel secure in its possession..."

Pescadero pioneer and blacksmith John Goulson read a poem to the happy picnickers. That evening there was standing-room only at the "Grand Hop", where an orchestra from San Francisco entertained the revelers, who believed their problems were over.

But while Assembly Bill #103 may have dedicated Pebble Beach to San Mateo County, it did not stop Loren from building his two-story Pebble Beach Hotel, the hoped-for rival of the Southern Pacific Railroad's elegant Del Monte Hotel, fifty miles south of Pescadero.

Contrary to his reputation, Loren spared no expense.

The Hughes Mill was manufacturing one hundred and seventy-three thousand feet of lumber for the hotel, which measured fifty by one hundred and forty feet. A ten-foot-wide veranda stretched around it. There was to be a one hundred-foot-long stable with stalls and sheds to accommodate guests with horses and carriages. Teams of horses were already hauling timbers to the site for the hotel foundation and adjacent barn, and piles of lumber were "assuming huge proportions".

With hard economic times in Pescadero, there should have been plenty of work to go around, but Loren was selective in hiring people, and he made sure that his favorite nephew, Carl Coburn, was one of those hired.

The villagers questioned how Coburn, then sixty-seven, could handle such demanding work. They thought "a younger man would be more successful."

After nearly a year, construction of the hotel was lagging behind schedule, but the development ballooned in scope. A clubhouse was proposed. A coursing track and a park for exercising horses had been laid out. Camping facilities with tents stretched out under ten thousand cypress trees planted as shelter from the heavy wind and fog, were foreseen. Cottages and more outbuildings were to be constructed. A plan to dam Bean Hollow Lagoon and to channel it into a fresh-water lake was studied.

During construction the road to Pebble Beach was open, and the two opposing stage lines feverishly competed, charging twenty-five cents for the round-trip from Pescadero.

While many resented Loren, others realized that the hotel represented a "new drawing card" for Pescadero. Now that other dazzling tourist sites such as Yosemite had opened up, fewer people were traveling to Pescadero. Reports of the Pebble Beach "War" discouraged some. On the other hand, "If anyone wants to get out of hard-times regions," it was said, "Pescadero is the place to settle. Don't mean 'boom', but steady progress of a conservative, safe kind. We may get a railroad yet."

Surprisingly, now that the Pebble Beach Bill had been signed into law, Pescaderans were in agreement that the smallest improvement, even by Coburn, could only mean good news.

But Coburn's investment in the hotel and the jobs that grew out of it were not appreciated by everyone. He was the target of mean tricks. One time "pranksters" turned on the faucets of his water-tank and let the water drain out. His brother-in-law Marraton was the subject of abuse, too.

At this time Dr. Emerson prepared Coburn for his wife's imminent death. The sad news hardened him for what he did to protect his property. He made a sign that read: *Pebble Beach Park—Private Roadway* and hung it over his newly-built road. Now everyone knew where he stood.

Within days, Loren's opponents made up their own sign that read: *Pebble Beach Park—Public Roadway* and hung it over the old cow trail. Six additional words had been added that amounted to a truce and a respect for Loren's wishes. They read: *Positively No Camping On These Grounds.*

The sign could have ended the Pebble Beach War, but then it mysteriously disappeared. The Pescaderans blamed it on "the dirty work" of Coburn's employees, and a warning was issued: "Perpetrators of such villainous acts are bound to be sooner or later known, and it will be decidedly unhealthy for them in this community..."

# SHOWDOWN AT THE GATE

The showdown at the Pebble Beach gate took place on a Sunday one year later. Loren Coburn, now sixty-eight, was driving a horse and buggy. With him was his sister-in-law Sarah.

"...[Supervisor] Adair came there with a party," sputtered Loren, "with the roadmaster and Joe Levy and quite a lot of people around Pescadero..."

It was clear to him that the ringleaders were going to tear down the gate and fence again. He fervently objected.

"He [Supervisor Adair] came there with a saw," charged Loren, "and sawed the fence right down and threatened me and raised his hand-saw on me and there was about twenty of them; and the roadmaster he was going to annihilate me...He was going to strike me. I told him he had better not strike me..." And then according to Loren, Supervisor Adair "cut that fence down and busted the whole thing open and went through..."

"...Sunday's the day for mobs," sermonized Sarah, who witnessed the damage to Loren's property. "...They get a mob up every Sunday almost..." She watched Supervisor Adair go "...right up to Mr. Coburn like this," she said, demonstrating by raising her arm and pretending to hold a hand saw, "and he said, 'I will saw your head off, old Coburn'..." Sarah praised Loren for keeping quiet.

"Well they came," continued Loren, "...and they cut the fences down, and went in there against my protest ...They said they were going to the beach...They said that they had a right...under the Board of Supervisors, that is, the County was going to open a road there."

Supervisor Adair hotly denied that he had said or was authorized "to open a road from the County road to the beach…" He had a right to be there, but he was not acting in his official capacity as a County Supervisor. The Board ordered Davenport Bromfield, the County Surveyor, to survey the road, he admitted, and he was to report his findings in November.

"…Adair said he should keep that fence open just as long as he lived," tattled Sarah, "whether he was in office or not…" She found it amusing, but not surprising, that his statements "that we should keep that fence down and keep it open" were made a "week and Sunday before the election."

"I told Mr. Coburn," said Adair truthfully, "that I would keep that gate open as long as I was Supervisor…"

The skirmish at the Pebble Beach gate began after Sarah said to Loren, "…There is a lot of barbed wire, your horse will get into that", and Loren returned to pick it up.

Just then an incensed Joe Levy came along in a buggy. Charles Pinkham, the roadmaster who lived in Pescadero, with Supervisor Adair seated at his side, drove up aggressively in a large County wagon drawn by four horses. There were twenty other men in the wagon as well as a plow and a scraper. Adair and Pinkham stepped out of the wagon.

"Coburn, get out of the road," ordered Levy. "I am going to the beach."

"I am not in the road."

"If you don't get out of the road, I will drive over you."

"You are not going through my enclosure to go to the beach." And so it went.

"…Adair got down from the wagon," recounted Sarah, "and he took a hand-saw and went to sawing the fence. Loren Coburn was standing between the buggy and the fence…"

"Mr. Adair, don't you saw down my fence," warned Loren.

"I will saw your head off, old Coburn," Adair allegedly threatened.

"You had better not do that…"

Pinkham swiftly stepped behind Loren and said, "I will smash your old head for you."

"I would not do that, Mr. Pinkham," said Loren.

"They turned around the buggy," narrated Sarah, "and told Coburn to get out of the way or they would smash the horses down. They finally backed the horse down, and they sawed down the fence and went through...And they took a plow and commenced plowing inside...and finally went off and left the fence down, so that the cattle came out into the highway..." Sarah added smugly: "They were very desirous for me to get out of the buggy, but I didn't get out. I stayed there..."

Supervisor Adair described the incident differently:

"...Mr. Coburn forbid me to open this gate or fence," he said. "And I told him I should do it, and I did it..." He said Coburn's horse and buggy blocked access to the gate and fence. The top of the gate consisted of a "plank that was two by eight inches fastened with eight-inch wire nails, and I saw I could not pull it off..." So he took his saw and cut it down. "As I started...Mr. Coburn grabbed me by the arm and pulled my arm back, and I pulled the saw out and I said: 'Mr. Coburn let me alone'. I never raised it in any manner on him."

Asked to explain why he had begun plowing in Coburn's enclosure, Adair said: "...Mr. Coburn himself, or through his agents, had had a trench dug that I should judge...was three feet in width and three feet in depth, just inside of the gate-way. Then he dug it up and had the dirt hauled far away." That meant that Adair had to have the ditch filled in once again, which accounted for the plow and scraper. He swore that no soil was removed from Coburn's ranch.

The Supervisor's fourteen-year-old son was at the scene, and Sarah charged that he was armed with a rifle.

Adair said this son did not own a rifle. He explained that his son "...and two other neighbor boys started from home with this gun that belongs to my older son. He is a man of twenty-four...He [the fourteen-year-old] borrowed this gun...and they went on down to the Butano Creek to shoot mud hens..." Then they saw the commotion at the gate and came to see what it was all about. Adair asked his son if the gun was loaded, and the boy said no. His fatherly advise was, "You take that gun and lay it alongside the fence. A gun in a crowd sometimes is a bad thing." The boy obeyed.

The fence that Adair had torn down was up the very next morning.

The tearing down of the gate and the fence was costing Loren dearly. He complained bitterly that some of his stock wandered as far south as Santa Cruz, and he had to pick them up there. "In fact," he said, "I never did get all of my stock."

Loren believed that the Board of Supervisors controlled "the people" regarding Pebble Beach and the gate. Adair was an instrument. Loren said that Adair came to Pebble Beach "…to smash down the fence…with his axe or saw…They cut the fence down and burned it up, and I asked them why they did it. Adair…said 'I am the only one that is causing this. It is by my authority'…"

Loren said that Adair and his posse "had a bad effect" on his terminally ill wife.

Adair described the one time that he went to Coburn's house on San Gregorio Street to talk things over. "…I politely asked him if he had heard the rulings of the court, and if he would not prefer to go down there and open the gate himself; and he became very wrathy and scolded…and I went away. But he said that the County had no right there and had been acceded no rights. He didn't remove the fastenings. I had them removed."

"If the Supervisor knows and believes that the road from the usual road to Pebble Beach is a legal highway, why not prosecute Coburn for obstructing the public highway?" asked the *San Mateo Times and Gazette*. "If it's the private property of Loren Coburn, what right has the Supervisor or anyone else to break down his gates, leave his fields open for stock to stray off, etc."

To resolve the issue, Loren sued San Mateo County. In early 1895 a restraining order made Pebble Beach off-limits to the general public. Good news, albeit short-lived, was telegraphed to Joe Levy's general store in April. Signed by attorney William Craig, who had represented Loren in the past, it read: "Citizens may immediately open and freely use the road to Pebble Beach…" Judge McKenna had ordered that the public could use the road and the beach!

It was assumed that anyone could now visit Pebble Beach. Having heard of the nasty litigation, people in faraway places believed the beach was closed or that if they went there to pick pebbles they might be shot. There had been a dramatic falling-off of travel to Pescadero. The lifting of the injunction had the power to change that; there was much rejoicing, and flags were hoisted again as news of the telegram spread through the village.

Now the gate had to be opened quickly. A crowd of villagers rushed to the beach for the first time since Coburn began his lawsuit. They hosted a "grand" celebration in the tradition of the Fourth of July. Cannons were fired and the people cheered.

But once again the celebration was premature. As soon as the last wagon had rolled through the gate, Loren locked it. The building up and the tearing down of fences and gates resumed at a furious rate.

Other unpleasantries occurred. R.K. Farley, who often trespassed on Loren's property, escorted three ladies to Pebble Beach. Before they could step out of the wagon they were reprimanded by a fulminating Loren. He refused to let them go to the beach.

During the heated argument between the two men, Coburn allegedly took a sharp knife out of his pocket and opened it in a threatening manner. He told Farley that if he got out of the wagon "he would fix him so he would never come there again." The genteel ladies were unaccustomed to hearing this kind of language. Immediately after the tense confrontation, Farley swore out a warrant for Loren's arrest on a misdemeanor charge.

Loren's wife, Mary Antoinette, was seventy-two when she died that year. The loss left the millionaire landowner in the house on San Gregorio Street with Sarah, Marraton, Wally, Ah Gee, and Anna Celestia.

It looked as if the courts would decide the Pebble Beach question.

But first Patrick Sinnott, identified as a land-patent expert, caused a brief sensation when he charged that Loren had acquired Pebble Beach by a fraudulent survey. Sinnott claimed to have uncovered evidence in the Santa Cruz County Recorder's Office that proved that the borders of the original Punta del Año Nuevo Rancho reached only as far north as Gazos Creek, about five miles south of Pebble Beach.

Loren and his partner, Jeremiah Clarke, a San Francisco attorney who specialized in land titles, had bought the Rancho from a Captain Isaac Graham in 1860. In 1852 Graham had bought it from the heirs of Simeon Castro, who acquired the original land patent from the Mexican governor in 1842.

Sinnott said that Captain Graham, a notorious liar, bribed a U.S. Surveyor to draw up a fraudulent survey. If true, the boundary line was extended north to take in Pebble Beach and the small Rincon de la Ballena Rancho, a land grant which disappeared altogether.

There were rumors that the land patent expert was going to make this startling announcement: Loren Coburn had no title to the Pebble Beach property; but nothing developed from this.

Meanwhile, to prepare for his case, Loren had a letter written to Henry Hanks, the former State Mineralogist, inquiring: "Do the pebbles on Pescadero beach come from the land, or are they cast up by the sea?"

Hanks wrote back that he had studied the beach in 1884 and issued an official report at that time. "The beach at Pescadero," he said, "has a wide celebrity for all the beautiful pebbles found there. These are nearly all quartz, agates, carnelians, jaspers, and chalcedony, of many beautiful varieties…" He explained that "the sea along the coast of California between San Francisco and Pigeon Point is encroaching upon the land. The effects may be seen along the Pescadero beaches and at the high sedimentary bluffs between Lobitos and Half Moon Bay. The bluffs along the beaches," noted Hanks, "exhibited an outcropping strata of washed pebbles, a portion of which had fallen on the rocks below." In his professional opinion, the pebbles on the beach came from the disintegration of the bluffs and not from the sea.

The stage was set for the case of Loren Coburn versus the County of San Mateo.

# COBURN VERSUS THE COUNTY – JULY 1895

"Do you know why this beach is called Pebble Beach?" asked John L. Boone, Loren Coburn's counsel.

"Because we have a vein of pebbles running right through the ranch. It runs two miles probably, or three, and abuts down on the ocean."

Coburn, then a spry sixty-nine, was the first to testify.

"A vein of pebbles in the soil of the ranch?"

"Yes, sir, right in the soil of the ranch."

"How deep in the soil?"

"Well...they come up to the top of the soil and then run down probably six or eight feet, as they strike the beach. How deep it goes down in, I don't know, but pebbles had been found half a mile from the beach." He produced a glass bottle filled with shiny pebbles. "There is a little sample of the pebbles that came out of the soil."

"You have handed me a sample bottle filled with pebbles. Where did those pebbles come from?"

"They came from the beach."

John Boone offered the bottle of pebbles into evidence.

"State whether or not such pebbles have any intrinsic value."

"I object," interrupted E.F. Fitzpatrick, one of the attorneys appearing on behalf of San Mateo County, "on the ground that no foundation has been laid to justify the witness in testifying to any questions of value."

"Overruled."

"They are sold for money, often," answered Loren.

"State whether or not you have ever sold them for money," asked Coburn's attorney.

"I never sold any, but I have known persons—three or four parties who told me that they had sold them for money."

"I move to strike that out," said Fitzpatrick.

"I could sell them, but I never have sold any," said Coburn.

In late July of 1895 witnesses for Loren Coburn and the County of San Mateo squeezed into Room 57 of the U.S. Appraisers Building on the corner of Washington and Sansome Streets in San Francisco. The outcome would rest on Judge Morrow's view of legal rights.

Representing Coburn was former Senator John L. Boone. His client's position was that the status of Pebble Beach as a State Park was unconstitutional. Appearing as counsel for San Mateo County were William Craig, frequently employed by Coburn, and E.F. Fitzpatrick. Pescadero's oldest settlers, including Alex Moore, I.C. Steele, and J.C. Williamson, traveled to Federal Court in San Francisco to take the witness stand against the man who had closed Pebble Beach. Sarah and Marraton Upton were virtually the only witnesses on Coburn's side.

The gross injustice that Loren felt he had experienced in the courts over possession of Pigeon Point, culminating in the tragic murder of Scotty Rae on the wharf, and the loss of trespassing cases convinced Loren that he "could not get any justice" in San Mateo County. That is why he took his Pebble Beach case to San Francisco.

Offered into evidence as Exhibit A were the original patent and a certified copy of the deed from Maria Antonio Pico to Issac Graham.

"Incompetent, immaterial, and irrelevant," objected Fitzpatrick, the County's attorney. "It purports to be a copy of a copy, and therefore it is not admissible in this case."

Boone reserved the right to produce the original of the deed if it could be found, and if not, to prove its loss and produce secondary evidence. Boone had several more certified copies of deeds from Pico to Issac Graham to Lloyd Tevis, the President of Wells Fargo Bank and a director of the Southern Pacific Railroad, to J.B. Crockett to John Baird to Jeremiah Clarke, Coburn's partner, and finally to Loren Coburn in 1865.

Coburn had continuously maintained the property and paid the property taxes.

"Of course we have parted with some of it," noted Loren, referring to the sale of land to the prominent Steele family.

"State whether or not if any County road passes through that piece of land...," Boone asked, meaning the land near Pebble Beach.

"There is a County road running from Pescadero to Santa Cruz. It runs the whole length of the grant."

"...How far on an average from the seashore does that road go through the ranch?"

"Well, in some places it is nearly a mile between the road and the sea, and then in some places not more than a quarter of a mile..."

"What is the length of the ranch from one end to the other?..."

Coburn estimated twelve or fourteen miles, "...about seventeen thousand acres—a four-league grant." The land was subdivided into five hundred, one thousand, and two thousand-acre parcels and rented out to different parties.

"Have you any house or dwelling or building located on the western side of the road?" asked Boone, referring to the land near Pebble Beach.

"Yes, sir...I have got a dairy-ranch there; a house, barn, etc. I have got a stable and so on...The house is located right near the road..."

"Have you any road or roads—by this I mean private roads—leading from the County road to the dwelling?"

"There is a road which dairymen have always used to go down to the dairy from the County road...It is a private road...it has fences on both sides." Coburn said that he had maintained these fences for twenty years.

"What gate or gates had you leading from the County road into the portion of land lying west of the County road?"

"A private gate, such as we have had to lead to the dairy ranch, to go out and in, and take our produce..."

Later in the questioning Boone asked "...How long have those pebbles been found on that beach, to your knowledge?"

"Probably a dozen or fifteen years."

"Do you know how they came to get on the beach?"

"By the water of the ocean—the tides, and so on, washing them."

"Just describe the process by which the pebbles are washed on the beach and where they are taken from."

"From the mainland, by the sea washing up; the high tides up and down. They wash out from the bank. You can see them in the bank just the same as you can see them in the bottle."

"State what the effect of an unusual high tide is with regard to the quantity of these pebbles to be found on the beach."

"Well, a high tide washes them down, and washes them back up and takes them from the bank and washes them into the sea, and when the tide comes in from the sea it takes them back."

"State whether or not there is a larger quantity to be found after there is a high tide than there is after a low tide."

"Yes, sir, a larger quantity, a much larger quantity..."

"State whether or not you have had any difficulty with any one in San Mateo County with regard to the possession of Pebble Beach."

"Supervisor Adair has been down there breaking down my fences and bringing a mob there."

"When, give us the dates..."

Now Coburn seemed flustered and confused; he had trouble remembering and sputtered: "That must have been the time that he came there with about twenty of them..."

"Give us the time and place and the dates," coached Boone.

Strangely, Coburn replied: "That is something I have not got in my book just now...", and then his mind cleared and he said: "I should think it was about six months ago...Mr. Adair came there with a party—with the Roadmaster and Joe Levy and quite a lot of people around Pescadero." He then told the story of when Supervisor Adair threatened him with a saw.

"...[Supervisor Adair] stated that he had been authorized?" asked Boone sarcastically.

"Yes, sir...to open a road from the County road to the beach."

"Mr. Adair was there in what capacity?"

"He was the Supervisor…of San Mateo County."

"When he first came did he say anything to you or ask your permission…"

"Yes, sir, he said he was going through to the beach. I told him he had no right to go in there…Always whenever I put up my fence they would go through that same performance…Whenever I put up my fence they would tear it down…"

"How many times has it occurred?"

"Perhaps twenty-five times…" said Coburn. He mentioned that it caused his stock to stray off and that he had to post a guard at the gate.

"Now Mr. Coburn, how much have you been damaged by reason of the acts of those defendants?"

"I have been damaged a great deal…a good many thousand dollars…I don't think twenty thousand would pay me."

"If twenty thousand would not pay you, how much would?…"

"…If you take the Board of Supervisors as a starting point of all this thing, I have been damaged a great deal by the influence of the Supervisors…And I am sure by the Supervisors alone, I have been damaged ten thousand dollars."

E.F. Fitzpatrick led the cross-examination, asking about the controversial gate.

"Has there ever been a gate there?"

"…Ever since I had my dairy ranch there, " said Coburn.

"And that gate was unlocked during all those years, was it not?"

"I kept it for going to the County road and from there to the dairy."

"Was it locked or unlocked," pressed Fitzpatrick.

"Unlocked."

"Was it ever locked?"

"…it was unlocked generally for years."

"When was it locked?"

"It has been within the last year."

"It never was locked until that time, was it?"

"I don't know when it was locked or unlocked…"

"You never locked it until about a year ago," needled Fitzpatrick.

"No, I never locked it…"

"There was a well traveled road leading from that gate down to the beach, was there not, for many years?"

"…There was never any roads there."

"I said road."

"There was a trail," corrected Loren. "…I don't consider it a well traveled road." In his mind a private road became a public road when the public need for it was proven in court, the owner consented, the road was surveyed by the Supervisors, condemned, sold and paid for. To Coburn, the only road fitting Fitzpatrick's description was the present County road running from Pescadero to Santa Cruz.

"Is it not a fact," bellowed Fitzpatrick, "that there has been for over twenty years and is now, a well traveled roadway from that point down to the beach which you call Pebble Beach?"

"The public have been going there against my protest for twenty years…and they have made me a good deal of trouble." Nobody had a right to go to the beach without his permission.

"But they have gone, nevertheless, haven't they?"

"Yes and…I objected to it, and my tenants objected to it…," he said. The public "…would come in mobs of sixty or seventy and go through, and what could you do? One man could not do anything with a mob of sixty or seventy…"

Fitzpatrick proceeded coolly. "Is it not a fact that they would come over that roadway in question before you became the owner of the ranch?"

"Well, before I owned the ranch I could not tell. I was not there." There was a ripple of laughter in the courtroom.

"What was the appearance of this tract at the time you first saw it?…"

"It was a tract of country unfenced."

"…I mean what you have designated as the trail. Was that there when you first saw the ranch? What I call the road," he said, as if talking to a witness who was hard of hearing,"and what you call the trail...?"

"I don't know as there was anything there at that time, when I first knew the ranch...As far as Pebble Beach was concerned, nobody knew much about it. This matter was got up by a few speculators, picking pebbles to sell them, and stealing and picking up strawberries, and doing everything that is disagreeable, and I have objected to it a long while because they trespassed on me..."

"How many roadways or trails are there upon your ranch by the aid of which persons can travel to the Pebble Beach from Pescadero?"

"Oh...You can drive a buggy without any road from most anywhere to Pebble Beach...Sometimes they go on one course and sometimes they go on another. They go up and down and along the beach up and down the ocean. There is about three miles there that they go up and down."

"If you were to drive from the village of Pescadero directly to Pebble Beach, what roadway or trails are there over your land on which people travel?"

"I have a road built there myself."

"Now what other road is there?" asked Fitzgerald.

"There is no other road unless this trail that you are talking about, running from the County road down to my dairy..."

"I say are there any other roads that are traveled by the people?"

"I tell you they go anywhere," insisted Loren. "There are roads all over it. They can, if they can get through the fence, they can go most anywhere."

"How do they get in?"

"They break the fence...And they go right down to the beach."

"Is there a road there?" asked an exasperated Fitzgerald, but his uncooperative witness only replied that no roads on his property had been repaired by the County Roadmaster.

Fitzgerald switched his strategy: "How far beneath the surface is that trail, as you call it?"

"It may be four or five inches...It may be more in some places, and some places, less. They have run a little while in one track and then they would take another track...Within the last six months they have been trying to keep that particular place. They say the County has given them the right of way."

"How many years have they gone through that same aperture in that fence?"

"It has been twenty years since there has been a road down to my dairy."

"How long have they been traveling over these different trails, as you call them, to go down to the beach…"

"…for twenty years, when you come down to that…"

"This deposit of pebbles you have spoken of, Mr. Coburn, you say it extends through the soil of your ranch…a distance of half a mile or three-quarters of a mile to the beach?"

"Yes, sir, it runs more than that."

"These pebbles that you have produced here in hand, were they taken from the soil or from the beach?"

"Taken from the beach. But I have got some that were taken half or three-quarters of a mile from the beach, and then I have got some that were taken from the beach."

"Have you found them on the surface or did you have to dig down for them?"

"I have got bottles of them, and you can't tell which come from the beach and which come from the soil…"

"Did you have to dig down?"

"Oh, yes. I know the pebbles are there."

"You have actually dug down and searched for them," asked Fitzpatrick incredulously.

"There is a bank that I can see of them."

"I am talking about the pebbles half a mile from the beach."

"I dug those out myself…Maybe they go down a hundred feet…"

"How far did you go down?"

"I didn't go down more than five or six inches, because it was not necessary. They come right up to the top of the ground."

"And it is your opinion that they wash from your soil?"

"Yes, sir, I know they do," Coburn said confidently.

There was a collective sigh in the courtroom; many people present wished to believe that the pebbles were washed from the ocean onto the beach.

"You do not think any of these original pebbles came from the ocean?"

"No, sir, only what came from the mainland and went down…when the tide comes in extremely high it washes the ground and washes them out into the ocean, and then the water washes them back." Coburn tenderly referred to the Pacific Ocean as his polishing machine. "…You can go down and look for yourself," he advised Fitzpatrick, "and you will say the same thing; because it is nothing but rocks there…"

"There is a very well defined line," asked Fitzpatrick, "that you can draw in your mind, when you are upon the ground there at the beach where the pebbles are, and the place from which in your judgment they come?"

"…There is not a pebble there but what came out of the mainland…"

Fitzpatrick asked whether Supervisor Adair tore down the fence.

"He claimed to be the party. He claimed to be the man who had full control," stressed Coburn.

"Now, Mr. Coburn…I would like you to give me the items which make up the damage that you testified that you sustained at the hands of the County."

Coburn didn't have the opportunity to respond; the judge called the noon recess.

In the afternoon Coburn described the damages in a speech: "…It injured me…very materially in my business. People had gone all around telling about it, and they looked at me in a disrespectful way; and it has injured me not only in my business matters in that part of the country, but it has injured me in my family. It has injured my wife very much. My wife was sick along through those days. It had a very bad effect on her. And, of course, she was taken from me a short time ago.

"There is another thing," appealed Coburn, "…When a man's reputation is gone…it injures him in business matters. People think I wanted to get something that didn't  belong to me. Well, if that had been even true, I might not have had much excuse. But my property there, I claimed was my property—a Spanish grant. I had owned it for thirty years and had to pay taxes on it, and it is my own. If there is a pebble there that don't belong to me, then I have not got a dollar's worth of property on this earth. If those pebbles, and all those things down there on the beach don't belong to me and if I have not got any rights there, if they don't belong to me, and people smash in, and break in, and break down my fence, and signs, so they can go in there—they have destroyed my fence, and my cattle have run astray, and my horses, and I have been in hot water.

"You have no idea. Talk about ten thousand dollars! You couldn't pay me ten thousand dollars and get me to go through with that again. I would tell you to keep your ten thousand dollars and put it right back into your pocket. I wouldn't have it. I wouldn't touch it. I am talking truth. I don't consider ten thousand dollars would begin to cover the amount.

"Why, my wife—it troubled her…it had a great change on her. Everybody was against me. I hadn't done anything but what I thought was right. Why, I never saw a community act as they have done. The Board of Supervisors and the officers put them up to do that damage to my property. They are the officers of our County, and the people have said, 'Well the Board of Supervisors have said so, and there must be something in it.' Well, I say that ten thousand dollars don't begin, it would not begin to cover my loss…"

Unmoved, attorney Fitzpatrick said woodenly: "Is that your answer, Mr. Coburn to the question?"

"Well, what do you want me to say?"

"I asked you to give me the items which make up this ten thousand dollars."

"Well, haven't I given you some of them?"

"Then as I understand you, Mr. Coburn, you consider that your damage consists wholly in the fact that your peace of mind was disturbed?"

"No, my business…I have been running a stable in Pescadero. They have all gone against my business on account of this Pebble Beach."

"Why have they done so?"

"They have done so because they took a notion to."

"Was it because you shut that gate up that they did it?"

"It was because I didn't want them to go all over."

"Objection," shouted Coburn's counsel, John Boone.

"Is it, Mr. Coburn, by reason of the fact that you have run counter to the people there in shutting that gate up that they have not patronized your stable?"

"Objection."

"Well," answered Coburn, "...that may be a portion of it."

"Do you know of any other reason?"

"Well, they have been influenced by Adair, the Supervisor..."

"The people over there seem to be on one side and yourself on the other. Isn't that a fact?"

"Well they have been led a good deal by the officers of the County."

"Do you know that the Board of Supervisors have ever taken any action respecting your property?"

"Oh, yes sir...They have ordered a survey to be made there, and I think they have condemned a road..."

"Tell us what you know, not what you think," thundered Fitzpatrick.

"Well, I have been before the Board, and that is what Adair says, that he has a right to go on by instructions from the Board of Supervisors."

"Do you know of any official act...in reference to that ranch, or that road?"

"I know what he says."

"No, I say the Board of Supervisors..."

Coburn said that Adair told him of the Board's official decision to survey and build a road where the cow trail was located.

"Now, Mr. Coburn your livery stable is a small business, is it not?"

"Yes, sir."

"Outside of your farming and dairying operations, you conduct no other business except this livery stable do you?"

Coburn said he also raised stock.

"How large a town is Pescadero? How many people live in it?"

"...two hundred or three hundred."

"There are two livery stables in the town and yours is one?"

"Well, there is one stable there that never was a stable until this matter came up," he said referring to R.K. Farley, whom he had tried to have arrested for trespassing at Pebble Beach.

"You know a man named John McCormick?" asked Fitzpatrick.

"Yes, sir," admitted Coburn. "He has a livery stable…"

"He hires out rigs to anybody that wants them?"

"Yes, sir, occasionally when he gets a chance."

"Then the livery stable business is pretty well divided up?"

"Well, it is all pretty near one side. I don't get much of it."

"During the major portion of the year, there is not a very large livery business there, is there?"

"Well, there has not been such a great amount of livery business done these last two or three months, of course. Before that there was some business. That is, my stable ain't done very much. They have boycotted it." Loren described again the loss of his stock.

Fitzpatrick asked Loren to give the location of Pebble Beach.

"…Pebble Beach," said the witness, "is on a portion of a tract of about twelve hundred acres on the western side of the road running on to Santa Cruz and Pigeon Point and Butano Creek. The County road is the eastern boundary of that tract, and the Pacific Ocean is the western boundary…"

"You don't mean to say, Mr. Coburn, that the beach runs from the ocean back into your ranch, do you?"

When he answered that Pebble Beach and the ocean were on the western side of his property, was he also implying that the ocean and the beach belonged to him?

"How long…is that beach?" asked Fitzpatrick.

"Oh, perhaps five hundred feet."

"Isn't it three miles long? You said so in your complaint."

"Well, there may be pebbles along there for three miles. There may be a pocket down there. But what is called Pebble Beach proper is about five hundred or six hundred feet long. But they have collected pebbles along up and down there in other places."

"Is that Pebble Beach above or below high water mark?"

"Why it is above."

"Are you sure it is above the high water mark?" asked Fitzpatrick. If he could prove the beach lay in the high water mark, it would fall into the public domain.

"Are you sure you are sitting there?" said Loren caustically. "If you are, I am sure Pebble Beach is above high-mark. Of course I don't say that there don't a few pebbles come down into the ocean by the flow of the tide."

"Mr. Coburn," said Boone, beginning the direct-examination, "you say there is a road leading from the County road to what is known as Pebble Beach."

"Yes, sir, there is a trail," corrected Loren.

"How was that trail made?"

"Well, a portion of it has been by driving stock from different portions of the ranch to the dairy, and some people have traveled down through there. There are several of those trails, where people have traveled over the twelve hundred acre tract."

"What is the character of the surface there? Is it level or hilly?"

"It is hilly some of it, and some of it is not."

"How does this trail run? Direct? Or does it follow the windings on the level?"

"It follows the windings…they travel the most feasible road."

"Has there been any work done on that trail?…"

"No, not that I am knowing of."

"Then it is a way which has been entirely made by travel over the ground?"

"Yes, sir."

"Has there been any artificial assistance in any way?" Boone sought to prove that the road had not been repaired by Pinkham, the County Roadmaster, as a public road would be maintained.

Loren wasn't certain who did the work, but a little bridge had been built near the beach.

"Did you ever by any word or act make any donation or grant any right or privilege of way across the tract of land from the County road to the beach…"

"No, sir..."

"Did you ever build or construct in the line of that fence at any point, a free gate for the use of the public?"

"Never."

"Did you ever maintain, construct or have any gates in the length of that fence, other than such as were for your own personal use and the use of the persons holding and owning under you?"

"Objection," said Fitzpatrick.

"Not any whatever. I have had gates there, and ...I have had signs up there 'no trespassing' for years...they would tear them down."

"Did you ever have or maintain a gate in the length of that fence on the western side of the County road which you kept open permanently or temporarily for the use of persons passing through your premises?"

"Never, never in my life."

"...If I understand you, your objections to their passing through this gate and over your ground were strenuous, and that the people have become antagonistic to you."

"Yes, sir."

"And the County itself has attempted through its Supervisors to compel you to keep the gate open?"

"Objection."

"Yes, sir." Loren said he lost about five hundred dollars worth of stock.

"How much have you expended in attempting to recover and get back your cattle, after they have been thus let out of your premises?"

"Well, I have paid a man for going to Santa Cruz and getting them out of the pound there... twenty or forty dollars might cover that amount." Loss of his tenants amounted to about four thousand dollars.

"You say also that by reason of the antagonism of the people, caused by your closing of this gate, you have suffered in your business...How much have you been damaged on account of that?"

"...I should think one thousand dollars."

"What has been the effect of all this agitation and controversy upon your physical health?"

"Objection."

Loren, an inarticulate man, began another speech: "Well, it has very much—of course a man having as much trouble as I have had, with these parties, everybody against me, when I don't owe them a ten-cent piece, and they have got no reason for it, a man must feel a little bit—it had a very big effect on me, as far as my health is concerned; and my family, too, it has injured. Take it all through, I claim that money could not pay me…No, sir, money could not pay me. Take out your money and offer it to me, and I would say 'Keep your money. Put it in your pocket. I don't want it.'…" A few minutes later the gray-haired man with a neatly trimmed beard stepped down from the witness stand.

Two weeks later Loren was recalled to the stand. His attorney, John Boone, asked him for the original deeds to his land. He did not have them.

"…I now hand you a bottle containing pebbles," said Boone, "and ask you what those pebbles represent—where they came from."

"These came from the road."

"What road do you refer to?"

"The road running from Pescadero to Santa Cruz…"

"How far was that from the beach?"

"A half or three-quarters of a mile."

"Who gathered the pebbles?"

Loren said that he gathered them "right at the side of the road…"

Boone offered the bottle, marked Exhibit Q, into evidence.

"I now hand you, Mr. Coburn, another smaller bottle containing pebbles and ask you whether you can state where those pebbles came from."

"…Pebble Beach."

"How far from the beach?"

"Well, perhaps fifty feet from the water edge or a hundred feet."

Were they gathered from the beach or from the soil?"

"Right from the beach…I saw them gathered. I told my man to pick up some pebbles…"

The bottle was offered in evidence and marked Exhibit R.

Fitzpatrick began his cross-examination for the County.

"Mr. Coburn," said Fitzpatrick, "when did you collect those pebbles in the large bottle which was offered here this morning, marked Exhibit Q?"

"A couple of weeks ago—or a little more…I was riding out on the road, and I jumped out and picked those up…" He said his sister-in-law Sarah was with him.

"At what point in the road did you find them?"

"Well, about—I think pretty near a mile from Pescadero towards Santa Cruz, near Bean Hollow…"

"You say you found them upon the surface of the ground."

"Right on the surface of the ground."

"Was there a large bed of pebbles at that point?"

"Yes, sir. It crops out there probably fifty or a hundred feet wide."

"You say, Mr. Coburn, that you haven't made a search to discover whether or not you have the originals of the deeds, which have been offered by you and purport to be certified copies of the records?"

"Well, I looked over what papers I had there, and I didn't see anything of this kind…" With that Loren was dismissed.

Coburn's spinster sister-in-law, Sarah Upton, then fifty-eight, took the stand. She had known Loren for thirty-five years and lived in the same house with him for the past five years.

Asked whether she had seen anyone attempting to break through the fence at Pebble Beach she responded, "Yes, sir."

"Can you tell us when it was?" asked Boone.

She testified about the incident with Joe Levy and the effigy in 1891 and the angry confrontation between Coburn, Supervisor Adair, and Roadmaster Pinkham. She said that she feared for her brother-in-law's life.

Henry Hanks, the former State Mineralogist whom Loren consulted before the trial began, took the stand. Now a sixty-year-old chemist and assayer working in San Francisco, he said that he was the State Mineralogist for six years and that he examined, located, and described the character of the precious stones and the deposits in which they were found. He wrote official reports dealing with geological formations and locations. One report that appeared in the 1884 edition of the *State Mineralogist* considered the origins of Pebble Beach.

At the request of Loren Coburn, Hanks had visited Pebble Beach just two months ago. He said that he "…did not go down on Pebble Beach, but I went and examined the beaches north…and also the surface of the country and the character of the place which forms the bank of the ocean." He had made "a thorough examination" of Pebble Beach two years earlier, but he said he was unfamiliar with Coburn's other property holdings.

"I went to see the other beaches," he said, "on foot…I took the road leading to the Pebble Beach. I saw the gate; it was fastened, and there was a sign that warned people against trespassing on the road or using it, but I crossed the road. I had a right to."

"Was there any person's name attached to the sign?"

"I think Mr. Coburn's name was on the sign…Then I followed that road until I came to the ocean…That road follows a somewhat circuitous course…As you pass along that road you see the creek to the right…" He said that he did not go to the ocean but turned to the left until he came to the top of the bluff and examined it.

At this point Fitzpatrick picked up the cross-examination: "…this sign that you speak of, that you observed upon the fence, that was upon the last occasion you were there…last March?"

"Yes, sir."

"At the time you were there before did you see any such sign? The gate was unlocked the first time, was it?"

"I don't think I went down the same road…"

"That is," said Fitzpatrick, "the road you traveled over last March was a well traveled road."

"Yes, sir," agreed Hanks.

"A direct road leading from the beach?"

"Yes, sir, a County road."

They discussed the geological formations and Fitzpatrick asked, "…Now did I understand you to mean, Mr. Hanks, that the influence of the waves of the ocean acts upon this disintegrated matter which has fallen from the bluff and washes these beaches down from that point?"

"That is my opinion." Henry Hanks believed the pebbles originated on Loren's land.

"Then in order to reach these pebbles the waters have to run over the beach entirely."

"Yes, sir."

"Washing up upon this first deposit, this is the irregular mass that you referred to and which has fallen over the wall of the ranch?"

"Yes, sir. And that took place during heavy storms...It is a gradual encroaching of the ocean. The same thing is quite perceptible in San Francisco. The bluffs at Fort Point are constantly falling down, and the ocean is gradually encroaching upon the land; and as we understand by geological experience and say in geological parlance, the land is encroached upon by the sea, and afterwards, during other periods of time, the land forced the sea back by rising. But the coast, and in fact the whole surface of the earth, is constantly changing its relative elevation. During the present period the ocean is encroaching upon the coast of California."

John Boone asked Hanks whether he had seen "any evidence that would convey the impression that these pebbles were washed up from the bottom of the sea or brought there from the sea."

"No, sir, not at all."

Boone handed the former State Mineralogist the bottle of pebbles labeled Exhibit H.

"There is nobody," said Hanks, "could say those came from Pescadero beach, because there are other beaches on the coast of California that produce the same kind of pebbles."

"Please examine the pebbles contained in the bottle marked Exhibit G or H and see if you recognize those pebbles as being of the character of the pebbles found near the beach..."

"These are mostly quartz," said Hanks, "and they are of the general character of the pebbles found on the beach. If I may be allowed to say it,

I would like to give reasons why there are so many quartz pebbles there and not other pebbles…Quartz is so much harder than the other rocks that it resists the forces that disintegrate the rocky matter and it lasts longer; consequently you will find quartz where you do not find other pebbles. Other pebbles of the same size being softer, would be washed away in the form of silt. It is very common in California to find very large deposits of quartz pebbles and quartz boulders, and it has generally been considered a mystery why it is so. It is very simple, because quartz is harder and resists the action of the tides longer than other softer stones do."

Hanks was asked whether the pebbles in the bottle labeled Exhibit H had any value.

"They have no special value. They are only valuable as specimens, mineralogical specimens. Of course, they have a very slight value when they are polished and put in as jewelry, but it is the value of the workmanship more than it is of the material, because the material is very common."

Boone handed the witness a chain with stones.

"Supposing," he said, "those stones contained in that chain did not come from Pescadero beach, what would you then say as to their being valuable stones."

"I should think the labor that it cost to cut them and set them would be the full value that I would set to them…"

He was asked whether the stones had a special name.

He said no, but "they are formed in different colors…The presence of iron gives them a red color, and the presence of manganese would give them the color of amethysts. If brown they would be called by another name…" After examining the pebbles a while longer, he added, "…I should not call any of these agate at all. Then these are another variety of quartz, which is frequent, and that is jasper…No, sir I should not call any of those agate."

The testimony of Henry Hanks had punctured the myth of the beautiful, valuable pebbles found on the Pebble Beach at Pescadero.

Davenport Bromfield, the thirty-three-year-old former County Surveyor, was called to testify on behalf of Coburn. The San Mateo County resident had been working for the County and was ordered to survey a road to Pebble Beach in November of 1894. For some reason, by January of 1895 he no longer held the job.

Speaking of the Pebble Beach trail, Bromfield said, "…I was laboring under the impression that this was a County road…" In his work he was assisted by Joe Levy, Supervisor Adair, his son, and other citizens from Pescadero.

The County, led by Fitzpatrick, attempted to prove that Bromfield was surveying a road already in existence.

Later Bromfield testified that there was no gate when he was there, only an opening where twenty feet of the fence had been torn down.

Appearing on behalf of the County was "J.C." Williamson. The forty-four-year-old Pescadero merchant told the court he had lived in the seaside village for twenty-five years.

"How did you get to Pebble Beach when you got there?" asked Fitzpatrick.

"I have always been over what they called the Pebble Beach road," said Williamson. Along the County road which went to Santa Cruz, noted Williamson, and which bordered Coburn's ranch, stood a fence with a gate. The fence and the gate had been there for twenty years. "Up to about three years ago it was always unlocked…I have never heard of it being locked."

"What sort of a road is this one which leads from the gate to Pebble Beach?"

"It is a well defined, well traveled road. In some places it is worn down considerably, six or eight inches in places…It has always been traveled continuously."

"By whom?"

"Everyone that has been to the beach."

"What is there at this beach to attract a crowd?"

"Pebbles, small stones. It has always been a sort of public resort there ever since I have known anything about it."

"Is there any other place in that neighborhood in the nature of a public resort?"

"No, sir, none that I know of."

Boone now got his chance to cross-examine Williamson. "When did you first pass over that road opposite the beach?"

"Oh, it was a great many years ago. I think I went over it two or three months after I came to Pescadero, that is in 1869..." He said it was not fenced then, and was "...all open at that time."

"Do you know when it was fenced?"

"I think it was 1873 or 1874..."

"Has there always been a gate since that fence was constructed?"

"Yes, sir."

"This gate has been kept closed always, has it not?"

"Yes, sir, as far as I know. That is, it was closed the same as any gate would be."

"When you went there you would get down and open the gate, would you?"

"Yes, sir."

"And when you passed through, you closed the gate?"

"Yes, sir." Williamson said that work had been done on the road, "...a little done by different parties, but I can't say by whom...I know that the stablemen there had repaired some of the holes; that is filled them up; chuck holes, as we call them...but the road proper...is in the same place that it has always been."

"You say about three years ago you found the gate closed permanently."

"It was not closed permanently. It was opened a short time after it was locked." He claimed to not know who locked it.

Williamson was asked if he was ever there "with a party" that tore the gate down.

"I was there...two or three years ago..."

"And you found the gate locked?"

"Yes, sir."

"And some of your party went to work and broke the gate open, didn't they?"

"They got it open somehow; I don't know how."

"Did they go and ask permission of anybody to open it?"

Williamson was forced to say, "I think not."

"What did they do to open it?"

"Well," hedged Williamson, "it was barred up, planked up, across from one post to another, and spiked together. It was locked and nailed. I think there was chains on it...About fifty people were at the gate."

"Someone of your party went to work and knocked down the braces that were nailed up?"

"Yes, sir."

"And there was a chain on it."

"That was what I understood. I didn't see any chain. That was off before I got there..."

"Isn't it a fact that your feelings toward Mr. Coburn are not friendly?"

"They are only as far as Pebble Beach was concerned; that is all."

"The people of San Mateo County are all opposed and feel bitterly against Mr. Coburn simply on the ground that he doesn't want them to pass over his premises to Pebble Beach, isn't that so?"

"...Well, they are pretty much all opposed to him on those grounds..."

"Why did you travel over this road to go to Pebble Beach?"

"I went down there for pleasure; to pick pebbles."

"Did you consider that you had a right to travel over the road?"

After several objections from Fitzpatrick, Williamson said that he used the road "because it has always been a traveled road ever since I have been there, and there had been no objection to traveling the road."

"It was not then for the purpose of annoying Mr. Coburn that you traveled over that road at any time?"

"No, sir."

Alex Moore, then sixty-nine, told the court he was a farmer who owned a "little" seven hundred-acre ranch. Moore said that when he settled in Pescadero in 1853, there were "maybe a dozen people there." He was perhaps the only Pescaderan who had contact with Loren in the early days. When he traveled to the city, Moore occasionally boarded his horse at Coburn's San Francisco stable.

Moore said he first went to Pebble Beach in "November, 1851, on a mule..." He and his brother were searching for a place to ship produce from, when they stumbled upon the pebbles.

Most recently Moore had visited the beach with Marraton Upton, Loren's brother-in-law. Marraton "...took me down this Pebble Beach Park Road...the private road..." which Moore rated as a "pretty fair road". But Moore had used the other road, the cow trail, many more times. "...That is the road that has been traveled for the last twenty-five or thirty or forty years...We could go whichever way it was most convenient to get there—to get to the beach."

Unlike Williamson, Moore said the Pescaderans "never traveled over any particular road...," but after the fence was built in 1874, "...and a gate put up...then they made a road straight" to Pebble Beach.

"Is that the first road?" asked Fitzpatrick.

"Yes, sir; it is the first regular traveled road...It is worn out a foot deep in some places."

On cross-examination Boone asked if Moore went for the pebbles.

"No, sir," he told the amused courtroom. "...I went because the balance went. I don't know what the balance went for."

"You went there because others went there?"

"Yes sir; that is it exactly."

"How often have you been to that beach?"

"I could not tell you, sir...I don't think I have averaged once a year."

"Did you ever go with a crowd to take down the gate?"

"I went there with a crowd once, and Mr. Coburn was ahead of us. We followed him..."

"Don't you know as a fact that some of the people that were with you broke the gate down that day?"

"Most undoubtedly. Mr. Coburn ought to know. He was there."

Boone tried to lay ground for the theory that a road could easily be worn by animals. Moore agreed, but added that it "…would take…some working of the sod…"

"People went in to pick strawberries…and camped there in places?"

"Yes, sir. Teams went all over."

"You have seen them yourself."

"Yes, sir; I have seen them…repeatedly."

The judge announced a recess.

Next to take the witness stand was Issac Chapman ("I always write 'I.C.'") Steele. The dairyman and vice president of the Granger's Bank in San Francisco was then seventy-six-years-old and residing at Año Nuevo. This was land that the Steeles bought from Coburn in 1872. Steele remembered that Loren's ranch was not fenced until after 1872, because that was when his lease with Coburn expired.

He told Fitzpatrick about the County road to Santa Cruz: "…for years," said Steele, "there was no laid-out road. The road was held under the Spanish idea, that when a road was traveled a certain length of time it was a public way…Afterwards there was a road laid out." He recalled the right-of-way, leading south to Santa Cruz, was purchased from Coburn and "…that it was laid out as a public road. The fence was built after he sold the right-of-way."

I.C. Steele visited Pebble Beach for the first time in 1863. "I was along the shore frequently in the course of my business," he explained.

"How did you go?"

He rode horseback over a trail "…and a trail was considered a road," he emphasized, "that is, if it was publicly traveled."

"Where was the road?"

"…Where it is now…"

"How long have you known the road that is there now leading from the Pebble Beach gate to the beach?"

"…It has always been traveled ever since I went there…since 1862."

"What changes…do you know of that have been made in that roadway?"

"…when the water washed out the gulch, it extended up into the land; and of course, we did on this road the same as we did on all roads; we went around ahead of it and back again into the road."

John Boone got Steele to admit that there was another trail near the controversial Pebble Beach road that could be used to reach the beach. But Steele countered that this other trail was really an extension.

Next to testify was Henry B. Adair, fifty-three, a Pescadero carpenter and a County Supervisor for eight years. He encouraged laughter in the courtroom when he said he had lived in the village for twenty years, three months in November "…if I remain that length of time." Adair had known Loren since he arrived in 1875.

"Have you ever been to Pebble Beach?" asked Fitzpatrick.

"…Sometimes I have been there a dozen times a year and sometimes a half dozen times a year…"

"And when was the last time that you were there?"

"I was at Pebble Beach last Friday."

"What road did you travel over to go to Pebble Beach the first time you went there?"

"Over the present traveled road…"

"What change or changes, if any, have occurred in that road since you first knew it?"

Before becoming a Supervisor, Adair was the Roadmaster, and he said: "…There was a bridge that I had put up a number of years ago, torn up by some parties, and some dead horse was rolled into this gulch…and the stench was unbearable, and in fact, it rendered the road useless to pass by, and everybody had to go around by the swale and then come back into this road again."

"Do you remember how long ago the first work was done and what it consisted of?"

"I should judge the first work was done twelve or thirteen years ago…In the line of repairs, generally in the shape of filling up holes…it has not required the amount of work that some other portions of the road have, but I should say that I have had work done, well, a dozen different times."

"What has been the condition of the gate...with reference to being locked or unlocked, fenced or unfastened?"

"I have never known of its being locked, or any attempt made to lock it until...1891..."

"In what way was your attention called to the fact of the existence of the lock?"

"Well, I was told that it was locked, and I went and saw for myself that it was."

"Was that lock removed?"

"Yes, sir."

"By whom?"

"Well, I have taken the lock off quite a number of times, and I have broken the fence quite a number of times,"admitted the Supervisor.

"Prior to the removal of this lock or the breaking of a portion of the fence where the gate was," inquired Fitzpatrick, "did you or did you not receive any order or direction from the Board of Supervisors or San Mateo County on this subject?"

"I think not."

"Mr. Coburn in his testimony here has said this: 'Supervisor Adair has been down there breaking down my fences and bringing down a mob there.' Will you state whether or not at any time you took a mob from any place to break down any fence or gate of Mr. Coburn's."

Heads bobbed in agreement when Adair quipped: "I didn't think Pescadero was composed of mobs..."

Boone moved to strike the answer.

"No, sir," answered Adair to the question.

"Have you ever by virtue of your position as Supervisor invited any person or persons to join you to cut down any gate or fence of Mr. Coburn's?"

"No, sir."

"Did you ever at any time take with you, for the purpose of removing any gate or any portion of a fence of Mr. Coburn's, your son armed with a rifle."

"No, sir, my son has never owned a rifle."

"Did you ever have any conversation with Mr. Coburn in the neighborhood of his gate which was removed?"

"Yes, sir…Mr. Coburn forbid me to open this gate or fence…At that time it wasn't a gate, it was a fence. And I told him I should do it and I did it."

"Was that about the extent of the conversation?"

"Well, there might have been something more on both sides,"joked the Supervisor. (He later said that Loren's former tenants, James Wilson and John Montevaldo, never complained to him about trespassers.)

A few minutes later Fitzpatrick said, "And Mr. Coburn has testified that this road, this Pebble Beach road which he calls a trail, has shifted from time to time, as much as three hundred to four hundred feet. Have you ever observed any such shifting as that?…"

"No, sir."

"What action has the Board taken with respect to this road?"

"The Board ordered this survey made…and ordered that it should be recorded in the road book of the County…"

Asked whether the Board had compelled Loren to keep the gate open, Adair said, "No, sir."

"I call your attention to the testimony of Miss Upton…" Fitzpatrick asked if it was true that he had raised his arm in a threatening manner at Loren. "Do you recall that action?"

"No, sir, not in that way…"

In a strange twist, Boone called Edward F. Fitzpatrick, the County's Counsel, to take the stand. Representing Fitzpatrick was William Craig.

"Have you not," pressed Boone, "since the commencement of this suit and within one month of this time, employed surveyors to proceed to Pescadero and survey the coastline, the shoreline of the Rancho Punta del Año Nuevo or a portion of it, and locate the survey lines on the western line of that grant?"

Fitzpatrick denied that he had, but that the County had employed two surveyors.

"Is it not a fact that they discovered that the survey line was out in the water?"

"No, sir," said Fitzpatrick.

"Is it not a fact…that you are suppressing evidence which you know exists as to the western shore line—the survey line—of that ranch?"

"I desire to answer the question,"said a dignified Fitzpatrick, "although I think it is an impertinent question…We have not suppressed any evidence…"

"It is a fact, however, that you have not produced them [the surveyors] as witnesses in this case."

Fitzpatrick was forced to admit that "It is a fact, yes, sir."

Could it be that Loren's land included famous Pebble Beach? Could it be that the ocean encroaching on the land, as Hanks had explained, swept away the western boundary line?

Judge Morrow was to weigh the evidence before rendering his decision. Meanwhile an injunction was enforced against anyone visiting Pebble Beach.

*In 1910, Loren Coburn, 84, and Sarah Upton, 73, exchanged marriage vows in San Francisco. The marriage was widely covered by the San Francisco Bay Area press.*

*Good fishing, the surrounding scenic wonders, and Pebble Beach were the magic ingredients of Pescadero's popularity as a resort in the 1890s.*

*Linking San Francisco with the isolated coastside, the Ocean Shore Railroad gave passengers a view of beaches rarely seen before.*

*To reach the seaside resort of Pescadero, pebble hunters endured a dusty stagecoach ride over the steep mountains.*

*Until "the Pebble Beach War" pitted the Pescaderans against Loren Coburn in the 1890s, the shiny, colorful stones attracted a stream of visitors.*

*Courtesy: Ron Duarte*

*Loren Coburn sold his land to the U.S. government for construction of the Pigeon Point Lighthouse. It was completed in 1872. The beautiful lighthouse still stands.*

*Courtesy: John Edmonds*

*The poker playing Judge Horace Templeton lost a bitter fight with Coburn over the Pigeon Point Landing.*

*The Landing at Pigeon Point, owned by Loren Coburn, was the scene of the bloody gun battle in the 1870s.*

*Courtesy: San Francisco Maritime Museum*

*A native of Vermont, Loren Coburn arrived aboard the* Panama *in San Francisco in 1851. Soon after, the livery stable owner bought 10,000 acres on the San Mateo County Coastside. From 1862 until his death in 1918, Coburn had a tremendous impact on the history of Pescadero.*

*Early in the murder investigation, Wallace Loren Coburn was a prime suspect.*

*Sarah Coburn was found murdered in her Pescadero home on June 4, 1919. No one has ever been convicted of the crime.*

Pebble hunters stayed in one of Mrs. Swanton's cozy cottages. The popular hotel
burned in the early 1920s.

San Gregorio Street. Note the historic flagpole in the forefront. For years it was the landmark
to measure distance from central Pescadero. The Swanton House is on the left. Carl Coburn's
candy and tobacco store, "The Emporium", stands on the right.

*The Ocean Shore Railroad never laid tracks beyond Tunitas Glen, north of Pescadero. In 1913 passengers rode the stagecoach to Pescadero.*

*In 1921, the Lone Pine Inn, the former Swanton House, burned. It was then owned by Dr. C. V. Thompson, longtime county supervisor, who performed the autopsy on Sarah Coburn.*

*A fire in 1926 destroyed many of the buildings on San Gregario Street (Stage Road today). Luckily, Duarte's Tavern was one of the few surviving buildings. It stands today across from where the Swanton House and Loren Coburn's house once stood.*

*Joe Levy, who ran the general store, had several confrontations with Coburn over the closing of Pebble Beach. They were competitors in the stagecoach business.*

*Riding the stagecoach from Redwood City to Pescadero.*

*Pescadero was a close knit village where nothing that Loren Coburn did or said was a secret for long.*

*It was said that Coburn's Pebble Beach Hotel was built to rival the famous Hotel Del Monte in Monterey. The success of the hotel depended on the arrival of the Ocean Shore Railroad.*

*Loren Coburn's adopted nephew, Carl, betrayed his rich uncle.*

*The Hotel Del Monte in Monterey was built by the Southern Pacific Railroad.*

*The Coburn house (above and below) as it appeared the day after Sarah's murder in 1919. Wally "the Boy" Coburn (right) was interrogated by San Mateo County District Attorney Franklin Swart.*

*District Attorney Franklin Swart was one of the first officials at the scene of the murder in 1919.*

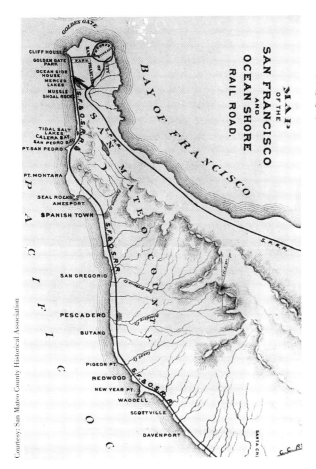

*The Ocean Shore Railroad never reached Coburn's hotel at Pebble Beach near Pescadero.*

*This Ocean Shore Railroad crew faced dramatic natural geographic barriers. Later, the 1906 earthquake inflicted grave damage.*

*In earlier times Pigeon Point was a bustling center of commerce.*

*This 1905 photo shows formations of thin bedded sandstone near Pebble Beach.*

*Marine View station at Moss Beach. Loren Coburn hoped the railroad would reach secluded Pescadero. He courted Ocean Shore Railroad officials, encouraging them to build a station at Pebble Beach.*

*Another view of the spectacular formations near Pebble Beach.*

# Coburn Mystery

## Amazing Document

### ...nd Principals in Latest Coburn Tangle

...the agreement and the attached notarial affidavit (below) purport ...ve been signed by Mrs. Sarah Satira Coburn.

Pescadero, Cal. June 18; 1915.

...ereby agree as follows: The undersigned,

...to pay to Mrs. S. S. Coburn the sum of

...if the said Mrs. S. S. Coburn succeeds in

...oren Coburn to sign an agreement to sell his

...One Hundred Thousand Dollars.

...burn agrees to do all that she can to induce

...to agree to sell said property. This refers to

...ranch and timber properties..

*Allegedly signed by Sarah Coburn, this document stated that she agreed to sell her husband's land for $100,000 to the mysterious Paul Guggenheim. It was a bombshell.*

*Archibald J. Treat was one of the many attorneys who represented Loren, only to later find it difficult to collect legal fees.*

*During the many court trials, Sarah Coburn was described as "a designing person."*

*J.A. Bardin, a Monterey County judge, and a friend of Sarah Coburn, was named in her will.*

*Sarah Satira Coburn's death certificate.*

PLACE OF DEATH, DIST. No.
(To be inserted by Registrar)

County of **San Mateo**

City or Town of **Pescadero**

Rural Registration District

**California State Board of Health**
BUREAU OF VITAL STATISTICS

**STANDARD CERTIFICATE OF DEATH**

19-026808

State Index No.
Local Registered No.

**961 167**

**FULL NAME** *Sarah Satira Coburn*

PERSONAL AND STATISTICAL PARTICULARS

CORONER'S CERTIFICATE OF DEATH

SEX **Female** | COLOR OR RACE **White** | Single, Married, Widowed or Divorced **Widow**

HUSBAND or WIFE of **Late Loren Coburn**

DATE OF BIRTH **May 1 1840**

AGE **79** year

OCCUPATION (a) **At home**

BIRTHPLACE **Vermont**

NAME OF FATHER **Amos Upton**

BIRTHPLACE OF FATHER

MAIDEN NAME OF MOTHER **Lucy Sheldon**

BIRTHPLACE OF MOTHER **Vermont**

LENGTH OF RESIDENCE

At Place of Death **30** years

In California **50** years

THE ABOVE IS TRUE TO THE BEST OF MY KNOWLEDGE

(Informant)

Filed

DATE OF DEATH **June 3 1919**

PLACE OF BURIAL OR REMOVAL **Cypress Lawn Cem.** | DATE OF BURIAL **June 6th 1919**

UNDERTAKER **WESSENDORF & SON SANTA CRUZ, CALIF.** **699**

*For years the eccentric millionaire landowner was known as the most litigious individual in San Mateo County.*

# CHAPTER FOURTEEN

# THE COLOMBIA SHIPWRECK

While awaiting Judge Morrow's decision in Coburn vs County of San Mateo, the villagers were temporarily distracted from the Pebble Beach War when on July 14, 1896, the *Colombia* lost her way in the thick fog and was shipwrecked near Pigeon Point. The Pacific Mail Steamship became wedged between the rocks and the reefs.

From the look of the gash across the bow below the waterline, there were doubts that the ship could be saved. The *Colombia* appeared to be lying at anchor, but she lay about three hundred yards from shore.

After its first roundtrip voyage to Panama, the *Colombia* was a week overdue in San Francisco. On board were thirty-six cabin passengers, twenty-six steerage passengers, and a crew of ninety. No lives were lost.

Captain Clark had confused the Año Nuevo foghorn with the horn at Pigeon Point. Maritime experts wondered how that could have happened, since the captain had good charts pinpointing the exact locations of the two signals. It remained a mystery, but the dense fog played a strong role.

There was less than one hundred yards of visibility when Captain Clark went on watch the night before the wreck. The steel-gray sky made it hard to tell when the morning light came, but the two foghorns could be heard. The wind was blowing from the south, and the captain thought he passed Pigeon Point and that the foghorn he heard was coming from that lighthouse. Maybe he forgot there was also a foghorn at Año Nuevo, south of Pigeon Point.

As he sailed through the thick fog at fourteen knots, he heard a whistle which he later insisted came from the west. To give ample room he veered from his course, and five minutes later the *Colombia* headed straight into the breakers on the beach. He ordered the engines reversed, but it was too late. There was a loud crash and a frightening thump, and the *Colombia's* bow came to its final resting place on the rocky bottom. At once seventeen feet of water rushed into the hold.

When the shock came, the *Colombia's* reversed engines had slackened the speed, so that there was not enough of a blow to knock the steward out of the chair where he was having his shoes polished. The passengers behaved like heroes and heroines. Wilton Lackaye, a well-known actor in San Francisco, was dressing when the ship struck the rocks: "…I didn't feel the slightest bit alarmed; neither did my wife. She knocked on the door and said the ship was going ashore, but that there was no danger. I finished dressing, and just as I stepped out of my cabin door I heard a young lady say to her mother in the cabin: 'Mother, is my hat on straight?' I declare I never saw such a lot of women in my life. There wasn't a scream, not a faint, not a prayer…But to tell you the truth, I've seen more excitement at the ordinary fire drills on shipboard."

White-haired Captain Marner witnessed the shipwreck from his pinnacle at Pigeon Point. He saw the *Colombia* "lifted by the roll of the sea and dropped again, crunching and grinding its nose into the rocks". It was a painful sight for an old sea-dog who had sailed with the gold hunters to San Francisco in 1850. He talked like a man witnessing the death of a friend, as the *Colombia* "breathed out her life in great struggles with the waves."

"…She was up almost on dry land," said Marner, "and my foghorn blowing twice a minute all night. This is one of the queerest accidents I ever knew of, and I've been thirty-five years at sea."

Three tugs arrived at the scene, and at 6 p.m. Captain Clark announced to the passengers that they would be taken to San Francisco.

The wreck was a cornucopia for the resourceful Pescaderans, who even scooped up the small, green limes that swept ashore. It was so profitable, wrote one newspaper, that one salvager bought a new home in Half Moon Bay.

Cases of olive oil sold for one dollar per gallon. Hundreds of feet of gold and white molding from the steamer's staterooms made beautiful frames. Tons of copper wire were used for clotheslines in Pescadero yards—where bolts of satin, muslin, blue jeans, woolen blankets, quilts, and men's clothing were hung to dry. New hat racks, writing desks, and other furniture, courtesy of the *Colombia*, decorated Pescadero homes.

Several tons of eastern white lead, used for painting houses, were immediately sold for four cents a pound. Gardiner, the village painter, pronounced it "the best white lead" he had ever used. And that was recommendation enough for the villagers to give their old homes fresh coats of white paint. The nasty business of the Pebble Beach War was eclipsed by the new look of Pescadero, now dubbed "the spotless town".

Three months later the *Colombia* was dynamited. As a point of interest, it drew the villagers to the southern beach just as the shiny pebbles had attracted them to the Pebble Beach. It was decided that the shipwreck beach was "better anyway." The Pescaderans christened it Colombia Beach.

When Judge Morrow's decision was handed down, it was not what the Pescaderans wanted to hear. The Judge said that the setting aside of Pebble Beach as a State Park was constitutional, because the State of California had title to that body of tideland within the limits of high and low tide when unoccupied by private parties. The word "beach" meant a place between high and low tides.

Since no objection was made by the County when Coburn put up a fence and gate in 1874—and because twenty years later an effort was finally made by the County to declare the cow trail a "public highway"— Judge Morrow reasoned that the public necessity for a road could not be that great. He awarded Coburn damages to his property, including damages caused by Supervisor Adair. A permanent injunction was issued restraining all San Mateo County officials, agents, and workmen from any part of Loren's land, except that below the high water mark.

After hearing the decision, Loren built a new fence in place of the gate on the old Pebble Beach Road. The Pescaderans would park their horse and buggies by the Bean Hollow Lagoon and walk back to Pebble Beach, always staying within the legal tideland. If the picnickers used Coburn's new road, they were met by him at his livery stable. Loren, who had been called many names, now earned a new one: He was crowned Pebble Beach's "Mayor of the Burg". He picked up the new title when a camper learned that he had to pay a dollar for the use of a stall in the new Pebble Beach livery stable. To lodge his complaint against the high price, he asked to see the "mayor"—who, typically, did not refund a cent.

A prankster in town unscrewed the four wheels from Coburn's farm wagon and rolled them across the street. The locals enjoyed a comical scene on dusty San Gregorio Street as Loren's brother-in-law, "Whiskers", and his houseman, Ah Gee, were forced to chase after the runaway wheels.

"The crime should be condemned," opined the *San Mateo Times and Gazette*. "The perpetrators and abettors should be punished to the full extent of the law. That gives our place a bad name and lets the lawless element get the idea that such acts may be winked at by authorities, because the sufferer is not popular. Heat not a furnace for your enemy," moralized the editorial, "that it may scorch thyself."

# CHAPTER FIFTEEN

# A PISTOL AT THE BEACH

"If old Coburn comes around, I'll give him the contents of this," warned Mrs. Matthias Gray, the no-nonsense widow of a San Francisco music dealer, gesturing toward her satchel, and opening it to reveal a small pistol.

One week after the Federal Court order prohibiting San Mateo County residents from trespassing at Pebble Beach, Mrs. Gray rode to Pescadero. She reasoned that as a resident of San Francisco, the San Mateo County injunction did not apply to her.

R.K. Farley drove Mrs. Gray and her companions in a carriage drawn by four horses. As soon as the widow set foot on the pebbles, she was confronted by one of Coburn's employees. Alerted to the latest trespassing attempt, an angry Loren Coburn tramped down to the beach. He found Mrs. Gray casually strolling with another lady and two men on the carpet of pebbles.

"Madame," Coburn called after her, "don't you know you are trespassing on private property and there is an injunction against people coming here?"

Mrs. Gray did not reply, and she refused to give her name. Loren later said that Mrs. Gray drew the pistol, cocked it, and exclaimed: 'You old rascal, if you open your mouth again, I'll put a bullet through you.'

Fearing for his life, Coburn backed off and drove his carriage all the way to San Francisco to consult with his "big city" lawyer, John Boone. Loren complained that Mrs. Gray had violated the injunction and threatened his life when she pointed a pistol at him.

Boone felt certain that the troublemaker Joe Levy had something to do with the latest development.

The next day Loren and his lawyer arrived in Pescadero. Their presence and the prospect of action in the quiet village stirred up excitement.

Boone described the scene that awaited him in the village: "...I found Mr. Maxey, a tinner, shoemaker, and justice-of-the-peace all in one and one of Coburn's most bitter enemies. I demanded a warrant for the arrest of Mrs. Gray, but he refused to give it to me, until I threatened to have him cited for contempt. The constable kept out of town, and it was almost night when I succeeded in getting the justice to deputize someone else to make the arrest.

"This man hunted up Joe Levy, and the pair went to Swanton's Hotel, where they consulted with Mrs. Gray. I had before asked the Justice where he held court, and he had told me, 'sometimes in my house and sometimes in Druid's Hall.' "

At dusk Mrs. Gray was seen to slip into the Justice's house. "...Then Coburn, the two witnesses, and I," said Boone, "presented ourselves at Justice Maxey's house. He met us at the gate and refused us entrance to his private parlor. I informed him that as he made his private parlor a public office we were entitled to go in.

"Meanwhile a great crowd had assembled at the door, and it became very threatening. Someone called for a rope, which was produced. Then a demand was made for someone to make a noose with which to hang Coburn and his lawyer. That did not disturb us. Levy was inside with the woman, and when she was arraigned she pleaded not guilty..."

The trial was set for 10 a.m. the next day.

"That was a lively night in Pescadero," reported Boone caustically. "About nine o'clock a great crowd assembled in front of Coburn's livery stable on the main street. Pistols were discharged, stones were thrown through windows, and various indignities were committed. About the same time Coburn's brother-in-law [Marraton], on entering the town, was set upon and received a volley of rotten eggs. Many of them hit their mark, and he was a sight to behold."

On Saturday there was standing room only in Justice Maxey's courtroom. Mrs. Gray was defended by Noyes, a San Francisco lawyer. Walker, the

County's District Attorney, had been asked to observe the proceedings.

"…Justice Maxey," remarked Boone, "had sent out written notices to all of the ladies in town, saying that court would be held in Druid's Hall, and as there would be two San Francisco lawyers, there would be plenty of entertainment. Business was stopped, and the hall was packed. My three witnesses testified directly to the assault…"

The testimony of the three witnesses varied. Coburn swore that Mrs. Gray stood when he approached her. She stepped back two paces before pointing a pistol at him and said: "If you lay your hands on me I'll put a bullet in you." Coburn said that he took her seriously and sought safety.

A second witness, a person "all believed the most truthful", stated that Mrs. Gray was sitting or kneeling on the pebbles when Coburn approached her. She quickly grasped a revolver from her satchel, pointed it at him, and made her statement.

The third witness, one of Coburn's employees, stated that Mrs. Gray stood and stepped forward two paces when delivering her speech, which included the clause: "If you approach me closer…"

Then Noyes, Mrs. Gray's lawyer, moved to dismiss the charge, first on the ground that Boone had not proven that the pistol was loaded, and secondly because there was no proof of criminal intent.

"I easily disposed of the first point, when, to my surprise," said Boone, "District Attorney Walker rose and addressed the court. He opened by saying: "I am sorry to have to recommend that the charge be dismissed, as the testimony shows that when the woman presented the pistol she said, 'If you say another word I will shoot you'. It was used as a warning, and as Coburn minded it, he was in no danger. The people of Pescadero and Pebble Beach have a perfect right to go on Pebble Beach when they please," exclaimed the District Attorney.

When Walker told the court that Loren had no right to order anyone off Pebble Beach, for it belonged to San Mateo County, "the very walls reverberated and trembled with the shouts and clapping of the assembled crowd, who represented the elite of Pescadero…" The audience went wild, with men, women and children applauding frantically.

The District Attorney advised Justice Maxey to dismiss the case. Coburn could not use the criminal process in the courts of San Mateo County to further his personal ends, said Walker, "by keeping people away from a place where they were entitled to go." No intent had been proven, and since there was no law against carrying concealed weapons, Mrs. Gray was acquitted.

"The feeling against my client in Pescadero," summarized Boone, "is intense, and I was not sure that our lives were not in danger."

After Mrs. Gray's acquittal, several wagonloads of ladies from the village headed for Pebble Beach to celebrate the victory. It was not known if they carried pistols in their satchels.

The newspapers demanded that the Pebble Beach War end. "If an immense tidal wave would engulf and destroy the whole beach," wrote one, "both Loren Coburn and the people of Pescadero would learn they could live without it…"

The tearing-down of fences and gates had come to a standstill, but the war was now one of words. In late August a Pescaderan signing off as "VIDOQ" snarled that "the capitalistic human octopus called Coburn was bent upon the ruin of Pescadero and its people". When the *San Francisco Chronicle* cast the villagers in a disparaging light, suggested that Coburn's lawyer was right, and recommended that Justice Maxey be removed, VIDOQ responded: "…Coburn…the man of thousands of acres; the man who, ignoring the outstretched hand of friendship, stands today a stumbling block to progress and prosperity; the man who despite his actions relative to the only spot on God's footstool that would make his name glorious among the philanthropists of the world and upon whose gray head the hand of providence has already been heavily laid, now stands before us with all the effrontery of a despot…And as he was heard to say 'I'll ruin the town', or words to the effect, we must admit he has partially succeeded. But when he uses or causes to be used means by which the people of Pescadero are placed before the public as illiterate, of low degree, and unworthy of the recognition of a respectable community, we feel it our duty to refute his statements, deny his rights, and with the belief that our words will be taken as the just uprising of a retributative and much maligned community, we leave the case in hand."

The Gray case weakened Loren mentally and physically. There was gossip that he had "baptized himself" by falling off the plank that served as a bridge over Pescadero creek. Carl Coburn, the surrogate son who lived across the street from his uncle and was now a college student, observed that Loren seemed disoriented. The Gray case also was fatal for Justice Maxey, who died from an illness associated with nerves soon after rendering his decision.

Communications did not improve between Loren and the villagers, but the telephone arrived in Pescadero. The office in Half Moon Bay was linked to San Mateo by "open wire", a source of maintenance problems during severe storms. To get "long distance" it was necessary to dial "Central" at Pacific Telephone in San Mateo. One year after the Gray case, telephone equipment was carried into Pescadero and installed in the local post office. It would be twenty-five years before electricity came to the village.

# THE PEBBLE BEACH HOTEL

Coburn's "modern caravansary", the Pebble Beach Hotel, had not opened its doors. Out of spite, Loren vowed he would not open the hotel until the "foolish" Pescaderans came to their senses. Estimated to cost one hundred and fifty thousand dollars, the empty, three-story, hotel, with a wide veranda stretching around it, was dubbed the "White Elephant" and "Coburn's Folly". The villagers sneered that nobody could live in Coburn's hotel, even if it were opened in the grandest style.

A San Francisco reporter wrote an unflattering portrait of the empty hotel as the home of rats, a place nobody would want to visit. In the daytime it was eery to walk through the echoing chambers and corridors. Outside the wind howled and the waves crashed. The wind sailing through the vacant top floor sounded ghostly, especially when mixed with the cries of the bats and the owls that lived there.

Numerous windows on the ocean side had been broken by birds flying through them. Some windows were boarded, but still the wind swept through the halls and stirred up tiny tornadoes of dust.

Loren feared that the villagers might seek revenge by destroying the new hotel, and he hired a watchman named Patrick Regan to protect the building from being set on fire. Regan, who roomed in the stables, patrolled the building at night.

The bad press cast a dark shadow over the big empty hotel. Another story said the hotel was the only building for over a mile, and the beach nearby was bleak; barren rocks lined the shore. The hills to the east were described as wild and desolate. There was nothing inviting about the Pebble Beach Hotel that could compare with the Hotel Del Monte.

On the contrary, soothsayers predicted a "sure death" for those brave enough to wade in the ocean in front of the hotel. If not death by drowning, then serious injuries could be sustained from the jagged rocks and the untamed surf that crashed on the sandy shore.

But Loren was resilient. He was proud of the gleaming white Pebble Beach Hotel. The rooms were well-lit and good-sized; there was hot and cold running water. He continued with his plans for a resort. A race track was laid out. A large pavilion was planned. He built a dam across a creek a mile from the hotel so that his future guests would have the advantage of sea bathing. When the tide flowed in, the floodgates would close, forming beautiful little Lake Lucerne. His work was admired enough to be criticized—detractors said he should have built the hotel closer to Lake Lucerne, making it a more desirable summer resort.

There were those who felt that the prosperity of Pescadero and the hotel depended on an open road to Pebble Beach. "...Coburn is a very wealthy man," wrote the *Redwood City Democrat*. "He is nearly seventy, and he has it in his power to become a public benefactor and to be the most popular man in San Mateo County and at the same time make money for himself...All he has to do is declare this private road a public road and deed it to his County." The paper was certain this would end the war, and that "he will enjoy the peace of mind (which is worth worlds to a man of his advanced years and great wealth) and enjoy a monopoly of all business done at Pebble Beach..."

The ill-tempered Loren failed to cooperate. He did not declare his private road open to the public, although he did invite the railroad people to see his new hotel. A surveyor from the railroad was observed near the hotel.

Still "...sons and daughters of freedom...demand roads as free as the air they breathe," was the predictable cry of the Pescaderans. They were despondent over the drawn-out Pebble Beach issue. No arrangements were made to celebrate the Fourth of July. It was embarrassing that "strangers were forced to submit to extortionate prices for the privilege of standing their team in a barn so that they can pick up a few pebbles".

In the summer of 1896 picnickers who were hungry for "rubies, carnelians, and moss agates could only return with hands full of strawberries."

Predictably, the breaking-down and building-up of the fences and gates recommenced. Joe Levy led the opposition which stormed the beach again and again. "The Mayor" literally chased after visitors to Pebble Beach to collect his money for stable fees. Some picnickers avoided "the tribute" by driving a mile south, where they hitched their horses and walked back up to Pebble Beach.

The long recession that came in the mid-1890's left a residue of distress even in the small Coastside village. Many Pescaderans were unemployed. The conservative members of the community complained about drunks lying about in the village. "Who is responsible," they asked, "the man who drinks or the one who puts temptation in the way?"

By the late summer of 1897, thousands of gold seekers struck out for the Klondike mines in Alaska. One Pescaderan headed north in time to enrich himself with twenty-five thousand dollars worth of gold.

Loren's brother, J.C., and his twenty-year-old adopted son, Carl, talked about mining for Klondike gold but admitted they were too soft to make the hard trip. The local joke was that instead of getting up and going, J.C. and Carl "mined for gold at the mouth of Pescadero Creek".

The Pebble Beach itself was never far from anyone's mind. In an off-shoot of the lengthy Pebble Beach case, San Mateo County Judge George Buck awarded Loren eight hundred dollars in damages for allowing the County a right-of-way over the millionaire's land. The people thought that this would end the war. But Loren wanted more money, and there were delays, creating new frustrations. The people who now had "operating telephones" found that this new, instant communication only made them more impatient.

Finally, after instructions by telephone from Judge Buck to Sheriff McEvoy, the "private" road to Pebble Beach was opened to the public. People went wild with happiness; the old brass field piece was loaded to the muzzle and fired by an old veteran. Champagne flowed in the saloons, and cigars were liberally dispensed. For days people flocked to the formerly war-torn beach, where they rekindled fond memories of the simple pleasure that picking up pretty pebbles had once brought them. During these years that the Pebble Beach War had raged, life had become more complicated, and the United States had emerged as a world power.

Casting a dark shadow on this bucolic scene was the fear that Loren Coburn would seek redress in court, get yet another injunction, and appeal to the Supreme Court. The thought of more time in court caused further tensions in the village.

J.C. Williamson had just posted the latest news of the Spanish-American War in his store, when Loren walked in. When he saw Mrs. Wilson, the wife of a former tenant, Loren allegedly took out a butcher knife that he used for skinning cows and deliberately cut her hand. Her furious husband stormed after Loren, and a fight broke out, resulting in a black eye for Coburn. At a later date an argument over a lumber bill caused Joe Levy to shove Loren out of his store. During that altercation, Loren picked up a railroad fish plate, a heavy bar of iron eighteen inches in length, and tried to strike Levy with it.

Loren did appeal the Pebble Beach decision, and in 1900 he won further awards for damages, stemming from condemnation of the road on his property. The Pescaderans could drive to Pebble Beach, but Loren had lost the fight revolving around the issue of when a private road becomes a public road.

The Judge's verdict proclaimed: *The Pebble Beach Trail is a public highway because it has been traveled over for more than twenty years.*

# PART III

## CLOSING DOWN

R. Guy Smith

# CHAPTER SEVENTEEN

# THE NEW SUPERVISOR

Four years after Loren lost his most important court battle, his personal freedom was threatened—and from an entirely unexpected direction. A niece named Ella Wheeler, a woman who earned the unkindly remark that she had "a face that could not stop a clock", petitioned the San Mateo County Superior Court in 1899 to have her seventy-three-year-old uncle declared incompetent. In her petition she stated that Uncle Loren "was likely to be deceived and imposed upon by artful and designing persons".

Ella presented as evidence Loren's odd lifestyle for a man of his wealth. Beside the fact that he was accompanied on his business trips by Sarah, an unmarried woman, her rich uncle chose to stay in "cheap" hotels, a sign of his mental weakness. The niece asked the court to appoint a guardian, and the man she had in mind was his brother, J.C. Coburn, who lived across the street from Loren.

Evidently, Ella Wheeler, from Southern California, had been in close contact with the J.C. Coburn family, Loren's poorer relatives.

Outraged by the legal action, Loren called his relatives "damn swine and thieves". He had not seen this coming. He said they were interested only in getting his land, and, surprisingly, many Pescaderans agreed with Loren's assessment.

However, it was true that Loren was experiencing occasional "spells" of dizziness, spasms, weakness, faintness, and symptoms that resembled epilepsy.

There was a trial over Ella Wheeler's allegations. Wearing a swallow-tail coat and striped pants, his goatee neatly trimmed, Loren sat in Judge

George Buck's courtroom in Redwood City. His freedom was in the hands of the Judge. This time Judge William Craig, who was co-counsel for the County during the Pebble Beach case, represented Loren.

As usual, the Pescaderans attended the trial, but having triumphed over their former enemy, they now sympathized with his plight. Because the Coburn name was guaranteed to grab headlines, reporters were present.

J.C. testified against his brother Loren. He said that Loren did not know who owned or rented some of his properties; that he could not count a sack of grain; and that he suffered from debilitating "spells". Carl Coburn said Uncle Loren was irrational. Dr. McCracken, a forty-one-year-old native of Canada, who had been the master-of-ceremonies at the dedication of Pebble Beach Park to the County of San Mateo, suggested that Loren showed signs of epilepsy. Manuel Bennett, a Pescaderan, took the stand, but under oath he faltered, admitting that he lied when he said Loren was of unsound mind. As Bennett now changed his testimony and said Loren "is all right", there were angry shouts of "bribery" in the crowded courtroom. With that, the prosecution rested its case.

As Loren looked around the room, he stared hard at the relatives who had turned on him. Would it end here?

On his behalf, San Francisco and San Mateo County businessmen testified that the man on trial was shrewd and in possession of his mental faculties.

Loren's attorney, Judge Craig, pointed out that his client was not a proven epileptic, and that even if he were, it would not prevent him from carrying on his business. Craig accused Loren's relatives of conspiracy; they were in a hurry to inherit Uncle Loren's fortune. He recommended the action be dropped.

Judge Buck ruled out conspiracy. However, he believed that the relatives acted out of genuine concern for Loren's best interests and said that he could not declare Loren incompetent.

This was a partial victory for Loren, and in a rare celebratory mood, the frugal millionaire invited friends to join him at the St. Charles Tavern in Redwood City for drinks and cigars.

After the incompetency hearing, Loren's sister-in-law, Sarah, refused to socialize with the J.C. Coburns ever again. She insisted Loren do the same. He no longer talked to Carl, the adopted nephew he had hoped to groom to take the place of his retarded son. However, despite Sarah's admonishment, he did go for rides in his horse and buggy with J.C.—but he was discreet, and Sarah knew nothing about it.

Believing that the incompetency hearing was resolved, Loren returned to watching over his Pigeon Point interests, hiring a new caretaker, one Edward Gayety, who was in his late fifties. He also planned to open the Pebble Beach Hotel at last.

Meanwhile Carl J. Coburn's political star was rising. He was elected a school trustee, secretary of a club devoted to the conservation of fish and game, Justice-of-the-Peace, and he was a notary public. His competitor was Supervisor Dr. McCracken, who also enjoyed the political life. When, in 1905 McCracken resigned to accept the position of Tax Collector, there was a heated contest for his seat. In the running were two young Pescadero men: Dr. Daniel Blackburn, a popular dentist, whose wife Harriet would become the postmistress, and Carl Coburn. Carl was now a married man, age twenty, wedded to the pregnant eighteen-year-old Minnie, daughter of the Methodist minister.

It was Carl, the Republican candidate, who won the coveted appointment as Supervisor of the Fifth Township—that is, Pescadero.

# ARZO COBURN

*"...Mr. Littlefield called at my place of business about a contract in regard to Pigeon Point and also the Gazos Creek timber claim...Mr. Littlefield said he had him [Loren] over a barrel."*

*—Carl Coburn*

Lemuel Coburn visited his brothers Loren and J.C. in Pescadero for the last time. Earlier, he thought he had seen an opportunity for sales of his products to the expected railroad enterprise. As the president of a manufacturing company in Massachusetts, he could afford to travel, but his health was failing. His company manufactured trolley tracks, fire-proof sliding doors, "overhead carrying apparatus", folding card tables, and store ladders.

Two years later, while enjoying a coast-to-coast tour, Lemuel's son, Arzo, then forty-three, and his wife, Lucy, were the guests of the J.C. Coburns in Pescadero. In Massachusetts he had become president of his father's company; he was the director of a national bank; he belonged to the Second Congregational Church and sang in the choir. He and his wife, described as "the best-looking couple in town," were constant companions who enjoyed a full social life. A modern man, Arzo was one of the first people to buy a "funny-looking, horseless carriage."

Now a visitor in Pescadero, he saw that his Uncle Loren's life was in a general state of deterioration. His Pebble Beach Hotel had opened, but legal battles still consumed much of his time; using the court system seemed to be an addiction. This time Loren was feuding with Littlefield, a stage driver who had a shadowy relationship with Coburn.

Carl Coburn, who once greatly admired his uncle but now turned against him, claimed that Loren said Littlefield was "...robbing everyone on the stage line, and he [Uncle Loren] wanted people to get together and tar and feather him, and to drive him out of town..."

For calling him "a thief, land robber, and highwayman," Littlefield had sued Loren for slander.

The reason that Carl had this information is that in his former role as Justice-of-the-Peace, he heard the law suits that ended up in his courtroom. "...This enmity continued," said Carl. "...The suit referred toward trivial matters...under three-hundred dollars; he [Loren] would sue for a horse or cow..."

But the relationship between Loren and Littlefield appears to have been more complex. Apparently the stage driver got a contract from Loren to cut redwood timber along the Gazos Creek; then turned around and sold the lumber rights to another company. This prompted Loren to file a series of lawsuits that took years to resolve. Littlefield, with or without Loren's consent and knowledge, acted as his leasing agent—and he was taking a percentage for himself.

It was learned "...that one of the renters came to Coburn and made him an offer for a certain ranch. The price one thousand dollars," said Arzo. "Loren ordered Littlefield to draw up a deed and Littlefield wrote in twelve hundred dollars. Loren signed the deed...the renter divided up the two hundred dollar profit with Littlefield." A number of renters were paying the stage driver fifty or one hundred dollars for the "privilege" of renting one of Loren's ranches.

This was going on when Arzo came to Pescadero at the turn of the century. He said that his uncle seemed glad to see him, but that is unlikely.

"I first met Loren over in his office, at the stable," said Arzo. "Carl hired a pair of horses from Uncle and drove up to San Mateo and drove my wife and me down...to Pescadero."

When Arzo asked his Uncle if there was a charge for the team, Loren surprised him by saying, "Well, my usual charge would be eighteen dollars, but if it was not for the feeling inside I wouldn't charge you anything."

This "feeling", intimated Arzo, originated from the hostility which Sarah directed toward Carl Coburn's family. Of course when asked about it, Sarah said it wasn't so, despite the fact that since the incompetency trial, she had not set foot in the house across the street.

Arzo saw his uncle several times every day, at his office and at his house on San Gregorio Street. He never went up to the second floor, which was forbidden territory. There was a folding bed in the living room; he was told that that was where poor Wally slept. Arzo was shocked at what had happened to Wally.

"...The mental condition of this son...," lamented Arzo, "...was that he is an imbecile—that he is insane—unable to take care of himself... This boy was taken care of by the Chinaman; while I was there, the Chinaman fed him at the table—swore at him and scolded him." So accustomed to the routine, Loren seemed detached. "...I didn't see anyone in the house give him [Wally] any attention except the Chinaman ...and Mr. Upton..." Marraton Upton, then seventy-three, "...was drunk most of the time," according to Arzo. "I should say that he was not at any time in condition to take care of this boy..."

Clearly Arzo thought that much more could be done for Wally, with whom he had played as a normal child. He thought that the way the family lived was incredibly dreary and unnecessary for a man of Loren's wealth. Was Uncle Loren crazy?

"I noticed," said Arzo, "...the boy did not go out of doors at all while I was there, and I spoke to my uncle and asked him was he not able to go out and ride. I told him the air might do him good." Arzo asked if Wally had been examined by a physician.

"No," said Loren, who added cynically, "Do you suppose it would do any good?"

"How could you tell unless you tried it?...How nice it would be if Wallace could be helped physically so that he could be your private secretary and help you out. Why don't you try it?"

Loren closed the discussion by saying nothing could be done.

Not invited to the house was Arzo's wife, Lucy. For this lack of hospitality, Loren "…apologized…he had his insane son, and his brother-in-law and Miss Upton…," remembered Arzo.

Arzo told others, "The two sisters and the brother were down there a good many years, and they had jumped on him and kept him in hot water a good deal of the time, and he wished he could get rid of the whole tribe. He wished he could take Marraton off somewhere and drop him on the way."

Marraton was a nuisance, and Loren wished Arzo would take him to Nevada and leave him there. He was willing to pay anyone gold pieces to get rid of Marraton. His only fear was that he would come back like a boomerang. Arzo disliked Marraton because he did all the talking at Loren's house, and it grated on his nerves.

"You can see my home; it is a perfect hell all the time," complained Loren. "They are jumping on me—and my insane son; I don't know what to do." One day his domestic woes got so bad that he asked an employee to fix up a room for him at the Pebble Beach Hotel.

There was no relief for Loren. Marraton claimed Loren owed him back wages for sixteen years. Instead of his owing Marraton, retorted Loren, Marraton owed him. Filled with compassion, Arzo said his Uncle was "in such a condition: his insane son, that sick sister Celestia, and that drunken brother, he didn't know what to do. He had so much litigation on his hands…He couldn't entertain us. I said—that is all right."

During their brief time together Arzo observed his Uncle's "conduct and actions". Loren was his father's oldest brother, and Arzo admitted that he "had an affectionate regard for him…"

Still he questioned his Uncle's competency. Was the old man in such a state that people could cheat him?

His Uncle's diminished capabilities were noticeable when the pair rode to three of Loren's ranches, where oats, barley, and wheat were threshed.

"I will show you," said Loren, "how I count out my share of the grain." He told Arzo he took one-third of the crop, while the renter got two-thirds. The agreement stipulated the tenants were not to move the crop until Loren's share had been moved to the warehouse, and the tenant was to be present when the crop was counted. But no tenants were there on this day.

Then "…we drove out to one of the large piles," recounted Arzo.

"I will now show you how I count these sacks," said Loren.

According to Arzo, Loren counted up to 147. "…and he kept repeating 47, 47, 47." Loren couldn't count past that number.

Finally acknowledging his problem, Loren said, "Hold on."

"And when he got to 50, he kept saying 51, 51, 51." Arzo told his Uncle that he was "fooling" himself, but Loren remained confident.

"And when he got to the next one," complained Arzo, "he looked that over, and one other pile beyond that he looked over, and he took a little memo book out of his pocket, and I noticed…it was filled full of pencil memoranda…I saw him take his pencil and put down the figures three hundred, two hundred, and one hundred, and some figures at the top…I noticed that he didn't put down any names of any tenants, and I supposed that he knew them…Neither I nor my uncle, at any of these ranches, actually counted the number of sacks on the ground…He counted up to 57 and quit…" Before riding back to Pescadero, they visited another ranch, and Loren didn't count any sacks there at all.

Arzo learned that at pressing-time Carl Littlefield, the stage driver, and the tenants robbed Loren of his crop. His uncle should have an income of twenty-five thousand dollars a year, according to Arzo's figures, but "…I can't figure but a single year that he has had a net income of over two thousand dollars or twenty-five hundred dollars. What has become of the money? And the hotel? That has never paid him a cent…" Arzo pointed out that "…It is a common report everywhere in Pescadero that Mr. Littlefield is robbing him."

Loren's business practices became more baffling. He had a scale to weigh grain at Pigeon Point. "…Those scales," said Arzo, "were…used for weighing the grain that he shipped from the chute. I made an exam of those scales. I found they didn't weigh correctly; they did not balance. They weighed against Mr. Coburn…"

When he told Uncle Loren about the scales, Loren casually responded, "Is that so, I will have them fixed." Then he looked at the scales and walked away.

After the Arzo Coburns returned to the East Coast, Anna Celestia Upton died in Loren's house on San Gregorio Street, where she had lived for twelve years. When in better health, she had been paid twenty-five dollars per month to help with the housework. Now Loren would pay Sarah fifty dollars a month to do the housework. But his miserable household was only reduced by one.

# THE EARTHQUAKE

*"Pescadero is destined to be the metropolis of the Coastside...The eyes of the world are on Pescadero. When the railroad comes is the day prosperity will be at hand."*
*—Al Weeks, Pescadero farmer and "capitalist".*

The earthquake struck at 5:13 a.m. on April 18, 1906.

The Catholic Church slipped off its foundation. Plaster from the exterior of the Methodist Church rained down on the street; the schoolhouse was declared unsafe. Cracks appeared in the bridge over Pescadero Creek, and rivulets of water seeped out of the earth. Natural gas escaped from fissures in the ground. Medicines and toiletries toppled off the shelves and shattered on the floor of McCormick's general store.

But the worst news of all was what had happened to the progress of the long-awaited railroad. Construction of the Ocean Shore Railroad, scheduled to run from San Francisco through Pescadero to Santa Cruz, had begun, although the rails were still far from reaching Pescadero. Now it was stopped in its tracks.

At the dangerous Devil's Slide area, eight miles north of Half Moon Bay, the rails buckled and jackknifed over the cliffs hundreds of feet down into the Pacific Ocean. Expensive equipment tumbled into the sea as well. Certainly the earthquake damage had exacted a huge financial toll from the railroad's backers. But how much and how long would the results of this devastating earthquake hold up the construction of this new railroad?

# DETERIORATION

*"I own a great deal more land than I ever supposed I did..."*

— *Loren Coburn.*

Now as a County Supervisor, Carl continued to post letters to his cousin Arzo, describing in detail their Uncle Loren's failing business judgment. Anyone could take advantage of the old man, he wrote. Arzo should come again to Pescadero and see for himself that Uncle was losing his mind; it was easy to trick him into signing leases. In Carl's opinion, Loren was being swindled everywhere. The stage driver, Littlefield, was a good example. He apparently borrowed money from Loren but had to be sued for lack of repayment.

In Pescadero Carl Coburn was well enough liked, but the villagers complained that he had at least one bad habit: he borrowed money and did not pay it back. Perhaps that was why he needed the help of Arzo, a man with financial resources, who could help pay the cost of expensive legal fees should there be another incompetency hearing.

Carl was busy watching Uncle Loren's increasingly erratic behavior, and his graphic letters brought Arzo and Lucy Coburn back to Pescadero. They stayed with the J.C. Coburns for about three weeks.

Seated over dinner in the gloomy dining room dominated by Loren's big safe, Arzo was pleased to learn that his Uncle had built a large warehouse at Pigeon Point. This was a healthy sign, he thought.

On this visit he found "...the Chinaman taking care of the house and Miss Upton looking after the boy. When she was not there, which was a good portion of the time, she left the boy in the charge of Ah Gee and

Marraton, and the boy would be shut up in the house two or three hours at a time with no one tending him. The Chinaman would go up to the China House and smoke opium and drink China gin…I went in there one time and saw him smoking…"

Arzo had cause to worry when he surveyed the old man's vast land holdings. Conversing pleasantly in the buggy pulled by one horse, Loren told Arzo grandly: "I will take you down to my northern border and show you where my land begins." He bragged about the thousands of acres he owned; how he acquired them for one dollar and fifty cents to two dollars and fifty cents per acre; how he hung onto the land, had not sold it, and paid all the taxes.

When they reached the northern boundary line, Arzo was visibly amazed: "Uncle, you own all the land here?"

"I own every foot for eleven miles—fifty square miles of land. I have got the best kind of title to it; I have a Mexican grant…Why when the railroad comes down here it will be worth one thousand dollars an acre."

The words "Mexican grant" aroused Arzo's suspicions. What Mexican grant, he wondered, as he admired the fertile land—perfect for a new townsite.

"Does Miss Upton own any land here?" asked Arzo, because Carl Coburn had reported to him that she made an arrangement with Loren. And whenever Loren went to San Francisco, Sarah was always with him. He saw Loren "…hanging onto Miss Upton's arm a great many times…"

"Pshaw," Loren brushed away the absurd thought, "she doesn't own any land."

"Are you sure Miss Upton doesn't own any land?" persisted Arzo. He had seen a document recorded in Redwood City stating that Loren deeded to Sarah four hundred acres.

Then who authorized the deed?

"Don't you suppose I know what I am talking about?" said Loren. "How could she own any land? I haven't sold any land or given away any land." He repeated that he had the best kind of title to his land, a Mexican grant, and launched into a speech which his attorneys later found embarrassing and sought to discourage.

Had Loren forgotten that he bought the land third- or fourth-hand, and had no direct dealings with the Mexican government?

Loren said he fought for title to his land for twelve years. He was defeated in the lower courts, but when he got into the higher court, he coached his lawyer on what to say. Before the Supreme Court, his lawyer said: 'May it please your honors, may I ask a few simple questions?' They said, 'Yes, if they are proper questions.' 'May it please your honors, what state is this?' The Supreme Court said, 'That is a schoolboy's question.' I said, 'Am I entitled to an answer?' The court said, 'Oh, yes, the state of California.' I said, 'Thank you. Now may it please your Honors, who does this state of California belong to?' The Supreme Court said 'Another schoolboy question.' I said, 'Am I entitled to an answer on that?' The Supreme Court said, 'Certainly, that is a proper question. It belongs to the United States.' I said, 'Which is greater, California or the United States?' The court said, 'The United States, of course.' 'I thank you. Now may it please your Honors, isn't it a fact that in the days of Fillmore, Mexico, that great and powerful nation with a big army and mighty navy, got into an altercation with Uncle Sam over a few little lots? Isn't it a fact that Mexico, that great nation, owned hundreds of millions of acres of land she had no use for, and she said, 'Uncle Sam, I will tell you what I will do. I have got all these hundreds of millions of acres of land more than I want. I will make a contract with you to sell you these few millions of acres of land for a million dollars; but he says, we don't own it all; there are dots around over this land that are owned by Tom Smith and Frank Jones and a dozen other names; but he says…we promised that we would protect them with our mighty army and big navy. Now Uncle Sam, if you will make a contract with us and agree to protect us, we will sell you these one million acres of land or more for a million dollars, with the understanding that if you don't protect these grants they will all revert back to Mexico. Now, may it please your Honors, isn't it a fact that California, Oregon, and Nevada are populated with millions and hundreds of millions of people and hundreds of thousands of miles of railroad and become worth a good deal of money. Now is Uncle Sam going to give up all this territory to Mexico just because we don't protect these few little dots of John Smith, Frank Jones, and so on."

Loren finished his monologue by adding "McAllister and Tevis and Haggin packed up their books and left the court, and just thirty-three minutes from the time that he went in, my boy got his title…from Uncle Sam." So Loren said smugly, "I have got the best title there is to my property."

The story struck Arzo as a sign that Carl was right; Uncle Loren's mind was indeed deteriorating. What made matters much worse was that Loren repeated this tedious story several times a day.

"A great many times," said a disconcerted Arzo. "He would sit right down at the table while we were eating and then go over to Carl's office and recite it there…He did not appear to remember that he had already stated the story to me upon the same day…"

Once when Arzo visited Uncle Loren at the stable he motioned surreptitiously: "Come out here. I want to tell you something." They proceeded to the rear of the barn and entered a stall to maximize secrecy. There Loren whispered: "I own a great deal more land than I ever supposed I did…"

"How did you find that out?"

"…It is only recently that I found it out. I own now clear up beyond San Gregorio and Half Moon Bay, a mile and a half beyond Half Moon Bay."

"Do you own all the houses between Pescadero, San Gregorio and Half Moon Bay?"

"Sure," said Loren enthusiastically, "my Spanish grant gave the title to everything." He patted his nephew on the back, slapped himself, and laughed out loud.

"What are you going to do with all this property and the people who have lived here for fifty years?"

"I am going to give them a lease and charge them so much a month rent."

"You would have a very great income, but if you tried, someone would come down and hit you on the head with a club."

Loren pledged Arzo to secrecy; he must not tell anyone about owning more land than he thought, not Carl or Miss Upton or anyone else.

"I won't say a word, Uncle…," promised Arzo. Later he discovered that the secret wasn't a secret. Uncle Loren told anyone who would listen to him.

Arzo was appalled by other facets of his uncle's behavior. From letters written by Carl he learned that when J.C. was unconscious and believed to be near death, Loren refused to visit his brother.

Edward Gayety, the sixty-year-old caretaker at Pigeon Point, was at the Coburn house when he overheard Sarah insist that Loren not see J.C. "If you go over," she threatened, "you can never come into this house again…"

A few minutes later Gayety urged Loren to go over.

"Get her [Sarah] into the house and I will go."

To camouflage Loren's hasty departure, Gayety persuaded Sarah to do an errand for him. She disappeared into the house, but Loren did not go to J.C.'s house as he said he would.

Arzo learned that when a villager told Loren, "Your brother is not liable to live," his uncle reportedly responded, "Let him die and burn in hell for all I care".

During J.C.'s serious illness, Arzo footed the medical bills. "…I found I needed quite a little money to pay for my father's care," explained Carl Coburn. "…I wrote to Arzo and asked him if he would send me out some money to help do it, and Arzo sent me a check for five hundred dollars; all of this five hundred dollars was used for my father during that sickness." When another Coburn brother fell ill, it was Arzo again who paid the bills.

Dr. C. V. Thompson was twenty-six-years old when he met Loren. The doctor resided in a building not owned by Loren, but according to Thompson, "Mr. Coburn said he owned that building and told me that I must pay the rent to him…He would say, 'You should pay your rent to me instead of the man you are paying'. I simply told him that we would see about it, and then he would be satisfied and would walk out."

On another occasion Dr. Thompson said "…a man by the name of Upton had an accident, and Mr. Coburn came up to me and told me to fix him up, and he would see that it was right…"

"What are you going to charge?" inquired the penurious Loren.

"...I will make you a flat rate of fifty dollars."

"As long as it is not five hundred dollars it will be all right."

"And when I wanted Coburn to pay," complained Dr. Thompson bitterly, "he swore he never owed me and would not pay the bill...He said he was not going to pay the old dog's bill..."

In self defense, Loren claimed that Marraton was not as badly injured as Dr. Thompson claimed he was.

Loren Coburn was eighty-two in 1908.

By now Carl had convinced Arzo that their Uncle had lost his ability to reason. "...There are very few of the leases made by him," said Carl, encouraging Arzo to come west again in Loren's interest. "They are generally filled in by Mr. Upton when he is sober and at other times by his sister."

Had a plot been hatched against Loren by the relatives living under his roof?

Arzo, now fifty, agreed to come. He and Carl met in San Francisco, where Carl explained that Loren would sign any paper presented to him. When Arzo demanded proof, Carl arranged a special meeting at which Uncle Loren would be present. They met at Arzo's hotel in the City.

"Why, how are you Uncle?" inquired Arzo solicitously.

"Good evening Judge," was the unexpected response.

"This is your nephew, Arzo Coburn," stressed Carl.

Loren took a good look at his face and said, "Well, I am glad to see you," but he insisted on calling him "Judge".

No documents were signed that evening, but several days later another meeting was called at the Grand Hotel in San Francisco.

Arzo said that they "walked into the hotel office and Loren Coburn sat down in a chair. Carl stood by his side and said: "Here is the paper" and Uncle Loren took the paper. He didn't read the document that was a deed to City Hall in San Francisco.

"Where shall I sign?" asked Loren obediently.

With his signature the fake papers showed that the San Francisco City Hall had been deeded to one D.B. Richards, a name that was to come up again in the near future. It was a ruse, and it was the first time that Arzo witnessed Uncle Loren sign a document without reading it.

Carl handed Loren, for his signature, other documents including deeds for the following: ten thousand acres of Coburn's land to Edward Gayety; a deed to Al Weeks, a Pescadero pioneer for the Pocket Ranch; a deed to Dr. Banks for the schoolhouse property in Pescadero; a lease to M.J. Perry, a Justice-of-the-Peace, for the Catholic Church; lease of the Jefferson House block in San Francisco; lease of the Southern Pacific Broadway depot in Oakland, which covered an entire block; and a lease to the Swanton House.

Arzo was shocked and dismayed to witness the ease with which Uncle Loren signed these falsified pieces of papers without examining them first.

It seemed that Loren had lost his mind.

As soon as he got to Pescadero, Arzo sought out Marraton for confirmation. There were rumors that he plied Marraton with drinks on some thirty occasions while interrogating him about his Uncle's business practices.

He also talked with Sarah Upton at the house; Wally was with her. What worried both Arzo and Sarah was that somehow Carl had managed to get a power-of-attorney to transact Loren's business for him.

"...I told Miss Upton," said Arzo, "I didn't like the looks of things over across the way. By that she understood I meant over at Carl's office. I said...Carl had got a power-of-attorney over Uncle and...it was too great a power for anyone to have...She said, 'Yes, we understand so.' "

Neither Sarah nor her brother Marraton approved of the influence that Carl had over Loren. They wondered what other documents Carl had foisted on Loren. Had he signed away all his property?

Arzo decided it was time to take a serious look into the matter.

# CHAPTER TWENTY-ONE

# AN ATTEMPT AT PROTECTION

"I am not seeking the appointment by the court as guardian," explained Arzo in a statement to the *San Francisco Call*. "…I merely want to see my uncle prohibited from disposing of his valuable estate in a ridiculous manner. There is no question about his being incompetent."

Arzo had consulted with attorneys about having Loren declared incompetent a second time. It seemed to him that he could no longer handle his estimated one million dollar estate. In his petition Arzo asked that a guardian be appointed over the person and the estate of Loren Coburn.

When the newspapers got hold of the story, they asked for an interview with Arzo—identified as a "steel magnate", the director of two national banks, and a trustee in a savings bank.

"Only a short time ago," Arzo told reporters, "my uncle deeded away the rental of valuable school property at five dollars a month to a physician of Pescadero. Lately he has acquired the belief that he owns twenty-six miles of land along the coast, including the towns of Pescadero, San Gregorio, and to within one mile of Half Moon Bay; and he has executed leases to this property to residents of Pescadero, in spite of the fact that the property is not owned by him.

"Seven years ago, he gave the exclusive right to certain contractors to all the stumpage on four thousand acres of redwood forests at an exceedingly low price and with absolutely no limit. The contractors were finally enjoined."

# PART IV

## VARIOUS COURT CASES

Courtesy: *San Mateo County Historical Association*

# CHAPTER TWENTY-TWO

# THE COMPETENCY HEARING – WINTER 1908

Loren was well represented by San Francisco attorney Archibald J. Treat, forty-four, and Archer Kincaid, a Redwood City attorney, then in his late thirties, and a Democrat. The second incompetency hearing was held in Superior Court in the Oddfellows Temple, which since the 1906 earthquake served as the County Courthouse in Redwood City. Arzo's petition held that eighty-two-year-old Loren was mentally incompetent to manage his property interests, located in four counties. He was described as a man who had always managed his own affairs, yet now he was signing any deeds presented to him for his signature; he needed to be protected from "designing persons" such as Littlefield and Sarah Upton.

Attorney Treat, a cultured man who counted San Francisco painter William Keith among his friends, served on the Marin County Republican Central Committee. He lived in scenic Sausalito, belonged to the Mill Valley Country Club and the prestigious San Francisco Olympic Club.

Representing Arzo was the law firm of Ross and Ross and Jordan, Rowe and Brown. Ross and Jordan actually handled the case. Like so many attorneys, George Ross, fifty-four, had represented Loren in the past. Known as "the dean of attorneys in San Mateo County", Ross was a leading figure in Republican politics.

Wearing judge's robes was George Buck, sixty-one, who had presided over Loren's first incompetency hearing in 1899 and ruled on facets of the Pebble Beach War case. A native of Maine, Judge Buck had been a District Attorney and Superior Court Judge of San Mateo County. He was up for reelection and understandably sought to project a spotless image; one newspaper piece depicted the Judge as one who "has stood in the lime-light of public scrutiny, and at no time has even a thought of official unfaithfulness or neglect of duty been raised against him." His rulings were rarely reversed by the State Supreme Court.

Once again the Pescaderans, who pitied the poor old rich man, came to hear this latest travesty against Coburn, who could be seen sitting in the courtroom, looking alert and wearing a pair of boots made to order, typical of a real Californian. But there was less interest in this trial than the one nine years earlier. There was only one correspondent, who worked for a San Mateo County paper, and he was assigned to cover the case for the San Francisco papers as well.

From the first day the case smacked of a planned assault on the Pescadero landowner's fleeting reputation for sanity.

J.C. Coburn, now seventy-two, took the stand and rambled on about his wealthy brother's fading business acumen. He had resided in Pescadero for eighteen years, he said, and he announced to the court "…I formed an opinion of him nine years ago."

"Well…what is your opinion of his present condition," prodded Arzo's counsel, Mr. Jordan.

"…I think he is worse now than he was then. He is not competent…"

In other testimony, J.C. said "…So far as Mr. Loren Coburn's ability to get about is concerned, he is about as active and spry now as he was eight or nine years ago, only he goes a little lame more than he used to— bent over…" J.C. insisted that Loren "deeded some property to Miss Upton" during the Pebble Beach War and that he had seen the deed. Loren labeled it fraudulent, to which J.C. said "…go over to the Recorder's Office and see…I know it is on their records…" Loren did send Carl Coburn to look at the records, and there was such a deed on file, yet Loren would refer only to his grant from Mexico.

J.C. did not wish to be appointed his brother's guardian; he believed that Arzo or Carl would be better. "…I am not looking to see a guardian appointed over my brother here," he clarified, "for the reason that I am afraid that he will not remember me in the disposition of his property…I am looking to others, [because] he has got a vast amount of property and he is not able to look after it at all, and he is getting so along in years, that it looks to me as though he needs somebody to help him…"

J.C. admired the fact that his brother "…acquired his property through his own efforts." He knew it was difficult, if not impossible, for anyone to tell him how to run his business, yet Sarah and her brother, Marraton, seemed to have a powerful influence over him. That was the way he saw it. Loren "…is afraid to do things," said J.C., "afraid he will get scolded when he gets back into the house. I know this by the way he treats me in taking me out. He comes out the way where they won't see him, to get in the buggy and go off…Many a time I have told him, why don't you come up here and take me in before them. But he is afraid he will get a terrible scolding if he did…"

Corroborating the testimony that Loren could not count bags of grain, J.C. added that he exhibited poor judgment when it came time to send the grain to market for the highest price.

On the stand Arzo conceded that Uncle Loren was spry, in excellent health and of good character. He expected any man that age to need help, but he did not want Loren's liberty to be curtailed. He said "…I had very delightful visits to my Uncle and I grew to love him; I saw that he was along in years and feeble." What concerned him most was Carl's power-of-attorney, and that was one factor that motivated him to take legal action.

Arzo explained that what had brought him West was not to specifically take his uncle to court, but to conduct business for his own company—although Carl's letters had spurred him to check into his Uncle's business dealings. Once he arrived in San Francisco and learned what had been going on, he knew something had to be done. He shocked the courtroom when he told of helping Carl to trick the old man into signing fake leases. Several documents, including the lease for San Francisco City Hall, were admitted into evidence.

"I don't think he [Loren] is competent," concluded Arzo.

Archibald Treat, Loren's counsel, pressed Arzo for "the names of the designing persons whom you are petitioning to protect your Uncle from."

"…I don't have any particular designing person in mind," said Arzo, "I simply considered it my duty to take care of my uncle."

But it was well known that Carl had told Arzo "…the only designing person I had in mind…was Miss Upton…"

Arzo knew there had been a "feud" between the J.C. Coburns and the Uptons. "They call Uncle JC and his family one side," he acknowledged, "and the Coburns and the Uptons the other." He noticed that since Anna Celestia had passed away the Loren Coburns had been friendlier with "Uncle J.C.'s people".

Carl Coburn offered the most sensational testimony. When he took the stand, Loren's face flushed with anger. The trusted associate, the surrogate son would testify against his Uncle.

His wavy hair and his charming smile momentarily disarmed the courtroom as he divulged information about the fraudulent leases. Introduced as evidence were leases for the Swanton House stable and the Southern Pacific Depot in Oakland made out to Carl. But Carl engineered his own self-destruction when he was invited to tell all he knew about his Uncle's handwriting.

"I have seen Mr. Coburn's handwriting a good deal," said Carl. "There are peculiarities about his handwriting that I recollect. I think I could point them out…"

As he spoke it became clear that he had studied his Uncle's writing at great length. But for what purpose?

"…he makes two little dashes between the "L" and the "C"," said Carl, "when he writes L. Coburn. I think you will find that in almost every signature he makes. On some of his "L's" there is no top at all, that is, he will make a slight dash on the top and a rundown on the "C's" most always…"

The revelations astonished the courtroom.

"The "C"'s…are disconnected at the top—the loop," began Carl without a pause. "The capital "C" I have reference to. On the final "n" he makes generally a dash over the signature, that is a circle over the "n" a little sort of a tail, only the tail goes over the "b" he generally disconnects.

As to peculiarities about the running of the small letter together, if he is taking his time there is not, if he is in a hurry there is. It is a signature that is pretty hard to imitate. He doesn't always write them the same, running the letter together. If he is in a hurry, he generally mumbles them along."

The tension in the courtroom was not relieved as Carl's testimony shifted to his uncle's mental state. Carl testified that Loren's mental condition had deteriorated. "Loren never claimed to own anything except from the Gazos Creek up to the Butano Creek. About nine months ago, he came into my place one day, and he says: 'I am going to explain something now; I have known it right along, but I haven't had time to do anything about it;' he said 'I own right up to Pomponia Creek.' That is about three miles up the coast, and he got talking about that and kept on talking, saying nobody knew anything about it, but himself and me, and then he concluded he owned up to Long Bridge about nine miles from Pescadero. Then he got up to Lobitos, which is two miles further than that. This was a subsequent conversation. And during the last month or so he thinks he owns a mile north of Half Moon Bay...He said he would give leases. He went to people and told them not to sell their places, and he advised them not to buy..."

More shocking was Carl's candid testimony regarding the notes given to Carl by Loren for the purpose of bribing judges. The defense rigorously denied this and cited that while it was evidence of corruption, the notes had nothing to do with whether or not Loren was competent. Judge Buck overruled the objection.

As to the bribes, Carl claimed "...the only reason I did that was so he [Loren] wouldn't get somebody else to do it for him; I knew he would if I didn't agree to it."

Exhibit 11 was a list of judges to be bribed.

During cross-examination Carl told Archer Kincaid about Loren's mishandling of the Gazos timber litigation and the desire to fire his attorney, William Craig. All this prompted Carl to encourage Arzo to come out West; Carl admitted accepting several hundred dollar checks from Arzo to cover his own expenses during the trial.

Strangely, on this occasion, the witness did not point to Sarah as the "designing person" Uncle Loren needed protection from. He talked of Miss Upton's influence and described her as "very kind and considerate and deserving of the four hundred acres in question."

Carl reported a bribery attempt occurred during the Gazos timber litigation in San Francisco, when Loren thought he would lose the case. "…He asked me," said Carl, "to give Judge Buck one thousand dollars to decide the case in his favor…I told him I was a Republican and Judge Buck was a strong Democrat."

Carl told of Uncle Loren giving him a five-thousand-dollar note to bribe another judge. There was a suit being heard before Judge Henshaw in San Francisco, and Uncle Loren thought the judge would rule in his favor for such a bribe. Not having the cash on hand, he handed Carl a note for the amount and instructed him to see to it that the case be decided in his favor. The note was entered as evidence.

One newspaper reported that instead of making the bribes, Carl deposited the money into his own bank account and rationalized his actions by convincing himself that his millionaire uncle owed him the money for services rendered.

Carl told of tricking Loren into signing the leases in Arzo's presence at the Grand Hotel. "I drew up this lease to the land of the Jefferson Hotel [at Turk and Gough Streets in San Francisco] and had him sign it…He pretended to read it; by pretending, I mean he would hold the paper up to his face…turn it over and say 'Where will I sign?'…"

Regarding the controversial power-of-attorney, Carl insisted that he needed it to make grain deals for his Uncle in the City.

There was a heavy silence as Archer Kincaid shed more light on Carl's dark side by asking how Loren could have relied on a man like him. Seemingly unconcerned with public opinion, Carl grinned boyishly and implied that he considered his uncle's misplaced confidence in himself as further evidence of his incompetence.

But before he left the stand, Carl was forced to admit that Uncle Loren looked rational and physically healthy in the courtroom.

Other Pescaderans testified that Loren was not the man he used to be. Dr. Banks of Pescadero testified regarding Coburn's strange ideas concerning the acreage he owned. "…Mr. Coburn spoke to me several times," said Dr. Banks, "in regard to holding some Spanish grant. He claimed to own land including the town of Pescadero, in which town I own a lot. He informed me that my title to that lot was not good. At that time I was in ignorance as to the exact idea that he had, and I asked him for information as to why my title was not good. He informed me that when he purchased the Spanish grant…the grant covered the town of Pescadero, and that the parties that I had purchased my land from had no title to convey to me. I asked him what he intended to do about it, and he said that he would not molest me at the present…Then I spoke to him about leasing it; he said that he would gladly lease it, mentioning the sum of five dollars a month, as rental; we arranged a lease for one year on that basis…"

Edward Gayety, who managed the Pigeon Point Landing's shipping chute, said Coburn always negotiated an iron-clad lease with his tenants, but he bought "shoddy machinery" that cost too much to operate. Loren was a man who became easily excited and stalked off when a deal did not go his way, said Gayety.

The testimony focussed next on Sarah Upton and her power over Loren.

To help establish Loren's relationship with Sarah, the witness recounted a conversation at the Coburn house. "I had my hat in my hand…and Miss Upton looked at me."

"Penny for your thoughts," she said. "Is it something about me?"

Loren was present, which made Gayety uncomfortable, so he said "I will put it off for a day or two."

"Go and say it now," encouraged Sarah.

Gayety motioned "…There is Coburn there. I don't like to ask you right before him." He thought it was obvious that he was teasing."

I will go outside," volunteered Loren.

"Keep your seat," said Gayety. "I may want a witness. I will ask the question, and you can take it under advisement, but please don't put me off any more than eight or ten days, because I don't think I can stand it. I came in here, Miss Upton, to ask you for your hand."

He thought everyone knew he was joking. But Sarah took his words seriously.

"Mr. Gayety, you shock me," said Sarah.

"It is out of me."

"I will take it under advisement."

The spinster took the proposal seriously. Then Loren followed Gayety outside and said "…Marry her and I'll give her forty thouand dollars."

"Mr. Coburn," gasped Gayety, "you don't suppose I want to marry a woman for money, do you? Why don't you marry her?"

"I married one and I got the whole family."

The damaging testimony took its toll on Loren. His face showed the strain; he had good reason to be fearful his freedom was at stake. During the recesses he was intentionally rude to the witnesses who had testified against him. He later fired Edward Gayety, who subsequently lost his home. Carl stepped in and offered Gayety a room in the back of the Emporium, his candy and tobacco store, and allegedly said the arrangements would work "until we win our fight for control of the old man's estate."

A parade of witnesses, now on behalf of Loren's competency, took the stand. San Mateo County Treasurer P.P. Chamberlain said Loren exhibited the ability to control his own fortune. The cashier from the First National Bank in San Francisco stated that he took care of his end of business deals. San Francisco attorney and Judge William Craig; L.P. Behrens, a banker from Redwood City; a San Mateo County liveryman, and Sarah all vouched for his sanity.

San Mateo County lumberman William Hughes, who supplied the wood for the building of the Pebble Beach Hotel, lent insight into Loren's way of conducting business. "…If you undertake to beat him out of ten cents, he would spend five hundred dollars before he would let you do it…"

Following a ten-day delay the testimony resumed with Loren on the stand. He breezed through two hours of questioning. His attorneys had him recount his early days in San Francisco, encouraging him to explain how he arrived from the East Coast in 1851. He denied he had ever knowingly sold San Francisco City Hall or the Hotel Jefferson.

More important, he denied giving a general power-of-attorney to his nephew Carl Coburn.

The controversial power-of-attorney was in the writing of Judge Fitzpatrick (who had been the County's Counsel during the Pebble Beach War case). Pescadero's Justice-of-the-Peace, A.O. McCormick, complained that Loren was in his office ten times a day—a regular pest. Loren brought the power-of-attorney to him to be acknowledged, he said, and Loren read it in his presence before it was certified. Yet Loren himself denied knowing of a power-of-attorney which gave Carl or anyone else the ability to sell his property. His idea was never to sell his property.

"Did you ever knowingly," questioned Treat, "give a power-of-attorney to Carl, by which he could mortgage your property or sell your property or make promissory notes for you with such powers as those?"

"Never in my life…" spat Loren.

"And you never gave a power-of-attorney that would enable the person who possessed it to sell your property?"

"Never in my life," repeated Coburn, "and I wouldn't; I ain't quite so incompetent as that."

Then how could he justify signing so many deeds?

Loren contended that his affairs were complicated, and he had to trust someone, and that someone had been his nephew Carl. He admitted he often signed papers that Carl handed to him, because he thought he possessed integrity.

Did Loren fail to read these various fraudulent leases because he could not read?

When asked why he put up with his "perfect hell of a home", Loren threw up his hands and exclaimed: "What can I do?" He saw no way of evicting Marraton without hurting Sarah's feelings.

Loren explained his business practices: "I pay my bills…I deal altogether in cash…And I haven't got no partners; I ain't in any stock because I have got all the stock in my corporation myself."

He flatly denied the bribery charges. "If I ain't got a case that has got merit, I compromise or drop it. That is the way I do business… When I have got a case and know it is mine, I never flinch. I stand to it, the same as I did on my eleven years' grant; they fought me eleven years and beat me in every court…"

Rustling his sheaf of papers, Archibald Treat briskly asked, "Do you dress yourself?"

"Well I come very near it."

"Nobody helps you?" Treat breathed a sigh of relief; he had to steer his stubborn client away from telling that same old story about how he got the land title from the Spanish or Mexican grant.

"I haven't known them to help me."

"What time do you go to bed at night?"

"Well," paused Loren thoughtfully, "I go to bed from eight to nine o'clock; I have no chance—or no use for this off to theaters and gambling places and taking a drink and having a great time; I never do anything of that kind. When I get through my work at night, I go into my house; I have a fireplace and build a fire, sit down, warm my feet, rest myself; up and about eight or nine o'clock I go to bed; sometimes it overruns that, when I have something quite particular to attend to…" He rose at six or seven in the morning, he said; and the folks that know me, they know that I am out around attending to business."

"How about smoking? Do you smoke?"

"No sir, I have got no use for it. I advise everybody to let it alone; keep their heads clear and take care of their health…"

Loren's attorney put the spotlight on Carl Coburn. He wanted to know if Carl ever said he would assist his uncle in getting counsel.

"Yes, sir," said Loren, "he said he would."

"And did he say he would assist you to get witnesses to prove that you were competent?"

"Certainly."

"Did you rely upon his promises to do so?"

"I relied upon him in a certain measure; I looked after it in a measure myself, but I had some confidence in him."

Turning to Arzo's visit, Treat asked, "And what did Mr. Arzo Coburn say when he called on you at the hotel in San Francisco?"

"…I went up there and saw him a few minutes and he commenced to talk about my property; I thought he had better take care of his own property—to come about three thousand miles to take care of my property…"

As Loren recalled, he asked Arzo: "What is the matter with you?"

"…I will tell you," said Arzo. "You are in litigation over some timber land here." He was talking about the Gazos property.

"Well," grumbled Loren, "what of it?"

"…don't you think you had better seek a compromise and settle up?"

"Well, I have got nothing to compromise."

The jurors looked favorably upon Loren's quick responses, alertness, and small-town manner. If he were incompetent, it didn't show. On cross-examination, George Ross was unable to shake the witness's confidence. When confronted with the deeds, Loren only admitted the signature resembled his. Nothing else.

Arzo's attorneys lost this round.

Dr. J.W. Robertson, a recognized psychiatrist with ties to the Napa Asylum in northern California, took the stand. He had called on Loren several times at his Pescadero home and examined him twice. Minimizing his client's eccentricities, he marveled at the health and vigor of the eighty-two-year-old millionaire. A verdict of incompetency would devastate the old man, he said.

"If this old man were declared incompetent," testified Dr. Robertson, "I personally believe he would not live a year under that stigma."

He then interpreted his client's personality: "…He is not and never has been a man of any very great mentality—that is, he has always been one-ideaed, eccentric, and …peculiar…I don't think he has been what you would call an intelligent man…He has confined himself to his environment, has read little and thought little outside of the special work he was doing...I believe this old man has for years gone on in a straight way accumulating property by what you might call accretion and not by any great mental effort...I don't believe he was ever capable of what you call modern finance..."

Dr. Robertson tried to account for why this rich man chose to live without luxuries of any kind. Visiting him in Pescadero, he had queried, "...I understand you are a wealthy man...[Loren] said 'yes,' and I said, How is it you have a room like this? He replied 'Isn't this room good enough?' I said it is surprising that you should have a room like this. He looked at the bed and said 'This is a comfortable bed. Is it clean?' I said yes. 'Are these chairs comfortable?' Yes. 'What objections do you find to the room?' None...I asked him about his food. He very seldom spends over thirty cents to fifty cents for a meal. He says that all any man ought to eat is a plain beefsteak and bread and butter, with a little tea and vegetables. He said why should I go to one of these fancy places and spend dollars there. At first I thought that was miserliness," said Dr. Robertson. "I don't think so now. There is a lack of ostentation about the old man, and I think there is a whole lot of the milk of human kindness in him...In speaking of the incompetency proceedings and the necessity of preparing for his defense, he sneers at the idea, and he did then, and he does to this day..."

"...I don't want to spend money," Loren told the doctor. "...All I want to do is go on the witness stand and let the judge examine me for himself..." That was how Loren believed he would be vindicated.

Robertson noted the surroundings were "tidy", but the carpet was worn and faded.

Delving into what drove Loren to amass his wealth, he opined, "I don't think he is collecting it for any particular love of the money; but I do think he loves his land and likes to collect it together...This old man all his life has had that miserly habit of acquiring, acquiring, and to this day he is the same old man that he was fifty years ago." Proclaiming that Loren did not suffer from senile dementia, he agreed he had a poor memory.

His client possessed "a keen sense of justice," according to Dr. Robertson, "at least justice so far as it relates to him and other people…" He cringed at the thought of being deprived of his rights and having to ask a guardian for four bits for a meal and then being humiliated by getting only two bits with which to buy a dinner.

"If there be any mental depression present in this old man," continued the psychiatrist, "I found it in this, his impossibility to conceive that anyone could transact business for him…"

The psychiatrist agreed that it would be "a very serious matter" if Loren signed leases for Oakland or San Francisco property that he did not own and also forgot that he had done so. But if he lied about it, Dr. Robertson didn't consider that as evidence of incompetency. Nor did he consider it incompetency if Loren signed a paper presented to him by someone he trusted. He did not believe Loren would sign documents without knowing what he was signing, thus implying that forgery was at work.

One day when the spectators and witnesses filed out of the courtroom, Carl, smiling broadly, walked over to his Uncle and extended his hand. Perhaps it was an orchestrated moment to expose Loren as a man not in control of his emotions. Turning white with rage, the elderly millionaire snapped back his arm as if intending to punch his young nephew, but friends standing nearby restrained the old man. Satisfied with having made such a scene, Carl sniggered and retreated to the safety of Arzo and his counsel.

When the testimony resumed, Loren's lifelong friend, attorney Judge William Craig took the stand.

"And how well does Loren Coburn read?" inquired Archibald Treat.

"Mr. Coburn reads very badly, as do many old men. He reads very slowly. He hardly reads a paper himself; you have to read it to him and tell him what is in it, and he will sign it."

"And your opinion is that he depends upon the statement of other people?"

"Yes, sir, and he can be tricked very easily. I knew him to be tricked once, several years ago. But I overlook these things, because he can manage his property better than anybody." Judge Craig reported that since Loren was first charged with incompetency, he had increased his wealth by three hundred thousand dollars. "I wish I had his mental financial ability," he said.

The attorney's summation followed. Treat sought to gain the sympathy of the jury as he said "...some years ago his wife died; that he was very fond of her; that he was very fond of his son; that there being but little now left for him, he not being a man of large mental attainment or inclinations, he turned himself closely to business and to the accumulation of property and to running his ranches; that not having anyone to assist him, he was lonely to the extent that there was no one to whom he could give his confidence; that he had looked forward to his son as a man who would grow up and assist him; that he had litigation concerning four hundred thousand acres of land, that in that litigation a man had assisted him by testifying in his behalf and obtaining witnesses for him and that this had led to their becoming better acquainted; but that the man was the adopted son of his own brother; that he gave him his confidence, obtained his assistance, and there grew up between them trust and confidence, and who held, or purported to hold, his power-of-attorney to the deeds and papers concerning which you have been questioned, and that while he appeared to read those deeds, nevertheless, the fact is that this man reads badly, reads poorly and slowly, as evidenced from time to time when asked to read a paper, questioning the person who presents the paper to himself to read the paper."

He made his most emotional pitch on behalf of his client when he appealed to the pioneer in every juror: "...did you ever observe that like an old Californian, he has his boots made to order? It is almost characteristic of a Californian, those boots..."

Treat reserved special epithets for Carl Coburn, whom he labeled a "Judas come to life", a "snake in the grass", and "a man who was on both sides and still on neither."

On behalf of Arzo and Carl, attorney Jordan declared that his clients had only the best interests for their Uncle in mind and the friendliest feelings for "the old gentleman."

The decision handed down by Judge George Buck in March of 1908 surprisingly brushed away any inferences that Carl was taking advantage of his aged uncle. Carl had absolute power-of-attorney, said the judge, and was in a better position to make decisions. He did not name a guardian, and that was what Loren had dreaded most.

However, a few days later Judge Buck enraged Loren by appointing the accuser Carl Coburn as Loren's guardian. The nephew he had denounced as an "ingrate" during the trial would now control his vast estate under a seventy-five-thousand-dollar bond.

"In view of the appointment of Carl Coburn as guardian, we certainly shall appeal the case without delay," announced Archer Kincaid, "and meantime we shall endeavor to tie the guardian's hands in the management of the estate." The plan was to have a trust company of one of Loren's friends appointed as guardian, but the plan failed. The attorneys, citing six separate grounds, filed a motion for a new trial.

His mission accomplished, Arzo Coburn returned East.

Loren could barely control his fury, and he vowed revenge. He thought there was no justice in this decision.

# SYMPATHY

*"They are not as a rule property owners, but are mostly composed of a crowd that you will find hanging around street corners waiting for something to turn up…I am not hunting trouble, but am trying to keep out of it, and all I ask is peaceable possession of my property while I live…"*

*—Loren Coburn*

As soon as it was known that Loren lost the incompetency case, his debtors refused to pay him.

Reflecting on the incompetency case, some observers concluded that Judge Buck was guided in his decision by a belief that the defendant was being cheated by other parties; appointing Carl as a guardian was done to protect the old man. But this was difficult to believe after studying Carl's testimony on the stand.

From the East Coast, Arzo penned a letter to his cousin Carl: "…Well my dear boy," he congratulated, "you got just what you deserved, for you have acted on the square towards my Uncle Loren…It must have been a supreme moment in your life, one you and those who were there will never forget…We have done what we thought was right, and we surely will stand together as long as we live, for our only object in this great fight was to see that justice—the strong arm of the law—was thrown around our Uncle as his protector…" But during the appeals process, Carl's guardianship powers were severely curtailed.

The sting of the incompetency verdict drove Loren to chase picnickers off his land, conjuring up images of the old Pebble Beach War. There were reports that Loren, disparagingly dubbed "the capitalist", was laying out a town near Pebble Beach and preparing to sell lots at the site of the new city which would be serviced by the Ocean Shore Railroad. He planned to operate a street railway from Pescadero to Pebble Beach and to the clubhouse and boathouse at Bean Hollow, a magnificent setting for the sheltered, curved beach of fine sand.

On the Fourth of July after the incompetency hearing, J.C. Williamson, the esteemed general store owner, was locked in a conversation with three customers when Loren walked by.

"...I always thought you were crazy," called out Williamson, "and I think you are now..."

In turn, Loren chastised the local people as being too slow, thus leaving it up to him to build the "New Pescadero".

Not all the Pescaderans resented his vigorous plans: "Coburn, who is wide awake, says we must have enterprise. Other places are going ahead, and we must be in the bandwagon with the others. When Coburn starts anything, it may be depended on that he will carry it through to a successful finish. We wish we had more enterprising men like this," wrote one villager in the newspaper.

Loren hired Mr. and Mrs. R. Corey to watch over his empty Pebble Beach Hotel. Mrs. Corey, who was gaining the important reputation of "setting a fine table", listened to Loren's woes, as he poured out his problems with the incompetency suit and the relatives, whom he labeled "rascals".

Mrs. Corey recalled that Loren talked about how the relatives "...had harmed him...The old man really cried...and he got kind of angry about them. They had abused him so; and he said that he had helped his brother so much and given him property in Pescadero and fetched him out when he was poor...that Carl was not his nephew—he was a boy that Mr. Coburn had brought up, taken him when he was a little boy, and he said he tried to do with Carl what was right until Carl tried this game..." She was referring to the signing of the bogus leases.

"I informed him," added Mr. Corey, who talked with Loren infrequently, "that Littlefield [the stage driver] his employee was a crook. I really don't recollect what remark he made, but I know he made a remark to me in regard to his tenants. Says he, I know that there are more or less of them taking what don't belong to them, but says he, what's the use. Says he they are working hard…they have families, and he didn't feel like putting them to any trouble. Says he, I will have plenty when I am done with this world. I don't know how many times I had that conversation with him…"

For the first time in his life, Loren was attracting sympathy.

# ANOTHER CASE – FALL 1909

A year later the California First Appellate Court overruled Judge Buck's decision declaring Loren incompetent, noting that since Loren had no will at the time of the ruling, he could not make one if he were declared legally incompetent. The court ordered the matter be reheard. The older residents of Pescadero were now pleased to learn that Loren had another chance to prove his competency.

This prompted Arzo to come West again, but this time he rented a cottage across the way from the deteriorating Swanton House. It appeared he was going to stay awhile. He asked his attorney to appeal the court decision and to take it to the Supreme Court, but the State Supreme Court refused to change the decision.

This was the signal for Loren to sue Arzo in the U.S. Circuit Court for two hundred and fifty thousand dollars in damages to his business reputation and one hundred thousand dollars to his feelings. The lawsuit fueled Arzo's determination to collect further evidence of his Uncle's incompetency. "Swift-footed" Carl, who, it was said, invested in slot machines and dice games, helped by trying to convince Sarah to turn on Loren, but she refused.

On the horizon, there lurked a new incompetency hearing. But a different kind of event would take place first.

# A WEDDING – WINTER 1910

Loren, a stooped old man, and the homely Sarah, with her arm looped through his, met J. Early Craig at the Yosemite House on Turk Street in San Francisco on February 26, 1910. There was to be a wedding.

It was Craig whom the eighty-four-year-old Loren consulted regarding his marriage plans. Craig offered his best advice and said it was "all right if she was the right woman." Then Loren revealed the woman he planned to wed was seventy-three-year-old Sarah Upton, his sister-in-law and the woman his relatives believed was exerting the wrong kind of influence over him. Listing her good traits, Loren said she had been loyal and handled Wally the best. Craig told Loren to go ahead and marry her; he also made the arrangements for the wedding to take place two days later.

About this time Loren announced "The relatives will not get a cent. I have borne with their persecution long enough, and now I intend to fool their expectations. They ought to have left me alone; but as they saw it to involve me in all this litigation and have me declared insane, let them bear the consequences of their own acts."

The couple were married at St. John's Presbyterian Church, with Reverend Alexander Eakin performing the service. Guests were J. Early Craig's wife, brother, sister, aunt; attorney Archibald Treat; Loren's business agent, Isadore Levin and his wife, son-in-law, and daughter. The wives of Levin and Craig doubled as bridesmaids. Treat acted as one of the ushers. Three reporters covered the event, including Harry Davids from the *San Francisco Call*; the other two represented the *Examiner* and the *Chronicle*. Sarah carried a colorful bouquet presented to her by Craig, and she wore a beribboned bonnet and a severe, long black dress. The simple, small ceremony was soon over. Reporter Harry Davids remarked that Loren appeared embarrassed at his own wedding.

"...after the ceremony," described another reporter, " Loren chuckled grimly and took his wife's arm and prepared to leave the church...He bowed with old world courtesy, and his bride blushed and smiled—the only touch of romance during the ceremony."

"I look as though I could take care of myself, don't I?" Loren remarked after the wedding. "I feel as sound mentally and physically as I did forty years ago. Do any of you kids want to come out to the street and run a foot race with me? I expect to enjoy life for a long time yet."

Attorneys Craig and Treat accompanied the newlyweds back to Levin's house at 1060 Ellis Street for supper. There they toasted to the bride's good health. Craig and Treat walked with the Loren Coburns to the corner of Polk and Ellis streets, where the couple took the Polk Street car back to the Yosemite House.

"By marrying his sister-in-law," ventured an observer, "Miss  S.S. Upton, a spinster for fifty-eight years, who for the last twenty years has been his housekeeper, Loren Coburn, millionaire of San Mateo County... topped with a vivid climax last night a career which almost from its inception has been marked by a series of sensations and which in recent times has been hedged and beset by litigation between himself and relatives, brought about by the latter's efforts to have him declared incompetent..."

There was mention in one newspaper of Sarah having a moderate fortune, including real estate in Fitchburg, Massachusetts, valued at one hundred and fifty thousand dollars. Loren's holdings, according to this same source, included thirty-five thousand acres in San Mateo, Monterey, Merced, and Fresno counties, including timber land, "vast herds" of horses and cattle, and investments in industry. The entire estate was valued at thirteen million dollars, a highly inflated and erroneous figure.

The Pescadero band welcomed Loren and Sarah back home. There was a party at Loren's house on San Gregorio Street and an evening of dancing at the Oddfellows Hall down the road. A new relationship had blossomed between Loren and the villagers.

"I'll fool them yet," predicted Loren about what he would do to the relatives. "…The old man is not quite incompetent; he has sense enough to pick the best woman and his truest friend for a wife."

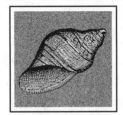

# CHAPTER TWENTY-SIX

# A PROPER WILL

Undermining everything was this disturbing letter signed by Mrs. Loren Coburn that appeared in the *San Mateo Times and Gazette*; it was an angry response to an accusation from Arzo that she had tried to make a compromise with him. "...in regard to Loren Coburn's property...I wish to say," she wrote, "that I never made any such offer, nor do I intend to, as who ever heard of Loren Coburn making any compromise with his dearest relations, when they tried to beat him out of his hard-earned property. I do say that his brothers have been trying to get me to go in with them for over fifteen years past and make Loren Coburn out crazy or incompetent and that they would agree with me, if I would do so, to give me an equal share with them in all the money and property that he, Loren Coburn had..." She ended by accusing Arzo of trying to make the public believe that everything he was doing was for Loren's "good".

Loren and Sarah kept very busy straightening out their affairs. The couple saw Judge Hebbard for advice about drawing up a will. "...If my son should die before I do," Loren reportedly inquired, "what would be the effect of earlier wills?"

"There is a chance," explained Judge Hebbard, "of its going to heirs other than your wife."

"I do not want that."

"Well, you can have another will, in which there will be a clause which will dispose of your entire estate as you desire. To whom do you wish it all to go?"

"If my son dies before I do, I wish it all to go to my wife," said Loren.

The will, made out by Judge Hebbard, dated April 14, 1910, left all the property to Wally and to Sarah. If Wally died first, all of it went to Sarah. The will was kept by Loren's business agent, Isadore Levin, in a safe deposit box. Executors were said to be Sarah and Levin.

Arzo was shocked to learn from Carl that Wally would inherit part of Loren's estate; it strengthened his conviction that his Uncle was incompetent.

However, Carl suddenly produced a second will, dated September 24, 1907, made out by a San Francisco attorney named J.J. Lehrman, who insisted that this will expressed Loren's true wishes. According to this second will, the income from one hundred thousand dollars was left in trust to Loren's son, fifty thousand dollars to Sarah, and the remainder was to be distributed to Carl's wife, Minnie, and the relatives on the East Coast. J.C. was the executor of this will. But the court proclaimed it invalid because there were no witnesses.

For the first time in his long life and to celebrate his marriage, Loren showed extravagance by buying a new five-passenger automobile. He announced he intended to enjoy life, since his "dear nephews" were so anxious about his health. The outdoor rides would add years to his life, he said.

But his litigation habit did not stop, and he continued to attack his former employee, the slippery Littlefield. There was talk that Littlefield and two associates were involved in a scheme to buy Loren's Monterey County land for two hundred and fifty thousand dollars and sell it for four hundred thousand dollars.

# CHAPTER TWENTY-SEVEN

# THE SECOND TRIAL FOR COMPETENCY – 1910

A short time after the wedding, Arzo Coburn again asked the court to declare his Uncle Loren incompetent. Treat and Kincaid represented Loren, and Theodore Roche and Matt Sullivan, a former reporter for the *San Francisco Call*, acted as counsel for Arzo. Judge Maurice Dooling of San Benito County sat in on the case for Judge George Buck who was said to be ill.

Before the case commenced, Treat was tipped information that two Pescadero ranchers, Jack Bennett and Robert Rownes, had been offered five thousand dollars to kill Loren and Sarah. The murder-for-hire plot, charged Treat, was initiated by people interested in Loren's estate.

Dr. Lustig, a psychiatrist with eighteen years experience, testified that he had observed Loren during the 1908 incompetency trial. In his opinion, the old man was of unsound mind and suffered from senile dementia. Dr. Robertson yielded to Lustig's position that Coburn had a poor memory, as many old men do, but firmly held to the view that he was not suffering from senile dementia.

While one of Treat's major strategies was to prove that Loren could take care of himself physically, Sullivan, the former reporter turned attorney, proceeded to showcase Loren's poor memory. He fired off questions about the wedding arrangements, the rooming house where Loren and Sarah stayed, lunch companions, his will, and the Gazos Creek litigation. He pressed the old defendant hard.

"I want to know," said Sullivan, "if you can remember this name. Was Roosevelt president of the U.S. during the Civil War?"

"Call it over and I will tell you what I recollect," was Loren's answer.

Calculating to unhinge the witness, Sullivan asked impatiently: "Was Theodore Roosevelt president of the U.S. during the Civil War, Theodore Roosevelt, the great hunter. Was McKinley the president of the U.S. during the Civil War?"

"I don't—it don't seem to me that is—it might be," faltered Loren, "but if you will call his name over—Lincoln; I think Lincoln was; Lincoln."

"You think Lincoln was president of the U.S. during the Civil War?"

"I think so," said Loren.

Sullivan launched into his line of intimidation. "Now who was the president of the U.S. during the Spanish-American War?"

"Well, I haven't kept any—I haven't had it in my mind. I am not exactly a politician, and I go in more for business than I do for politics."

"You are a businessman and don't take any interest in politics?" was Sullivan's haughty question.

"No. Politics I don't take so much interest in."

"Now do you remember what your father's name was, Mr. Coburn?"

"...My father, Ira Coburn."

"And your mother's name?"

"Mary Antoinette, I think," fumbled Coburn, naming his first wife.

"That is your best recollection?"

"I won't be positive."

"Did you ever hear of Clarinda?"

"Oh, Clarinda, yes, I think her name was really Clarinda."

Sullivan entered new territory, attempting to destroy Loren by exposing his extraordinary theories regarding the boundaries of his land. "Now, the question is, where does the southern boundary come, where does it lie?"

Loren made what sounded like a rambling speech, but it was the key to how he arrived at owning more land than he had originally believed. "Well I can't say, only I can say...I am entitled to thirty thousand acres —that is four leagues. If you say four leagues ain't but four thousand acres, why then you have to look at the record and see what that means. I claim a league of land is seventy-five hundred acres, Spanish leagues, old Spanish leagues. Those old Spanish leagues I go by, before the U.S. had anything to do with California or Nevada. It is just as plain to me as two and two is four. If it isn't plain I want a little information on why I am wrong."

Why had Loren decided that he should be translating acres into leagues? Leagues were the measure for the original land grants parceled out by the Mexican and Spanish governments of California. One league equaled seven thousand five hundred acres.

"Now all this litigation is a fraud," exclaimed Loren. "There is nothing in it. I ask for nothing only what belongs to me legally, what I am entitled to under the law—and the pretensions of incompetency, all that is all bosh. If I am incompetent, try me. I attend to my own matters, collect my own rents, take the money myself, and attend to my own business like any businessman and quite an extensive business too, and I think I ought to have a little protection for property rights. I pay my taxes every season, a good many thousand dollars. I am supporting my government, and I am entitled to protection. If I haven't got no show and haven't got anything to say, why I don't want to live in the U.S. I want to go to some other country where I can have some protection."

Loren was quizzed about the value of his land—where barley, oats, and wheat were grown—and his memory was tested when he was required to tick off the names of his tenants. Then Sullivan examined his aptitude for counting money.

"Now at the rate of six percent per annum...how much will the interest amount to in five years?"

"Well, six percent a year."

"On eighty dollars, yes."

"Six times eight is forty-eight. In how many years?"

"In five years."

"Forty-eight times five times forty-eight."

"Five times forty eight. How much is five times forty eight?"

"Well, I can tell you in a minute, I guess. two hundred and forty, is it."

"Two hundred and forty interest. Now you have got eight dollars," said Sullivan, confusing Loren.

"Perhaps I have made a mistake."

If the courtroom was listening to Sullivan, it appeared that all the tenants, including those at the King City ranch, had been cheating Loren. Sullivan wanted to air the embarrassing Spanish land-grant story, too, but Treat charged the petitioners were sneering at his client. Sullivan snarled that the association with Loren was affecting his mind. To stop the bickering, Judge Dooling called a recess.

When court was reconvened, Matt Sullivan touched a raw nerve.

"Can you read this and let me know what it is, this paper? he asked Loren.

"I don't want to read it," was Loren's strange answer.

"Read it yourself, Mr. Sullivan," shouted Treat.

"Mr. Treat, hold on a minute. This question is for Mr. Coburn, this being a deed from L. Coburn to D.B. Richards, of certain property in San Francisco—whether or not you signed."

"I never signed any such deed," said Loren gruffly.

"Will you say that is not your signature there?"

"I say that is a fraud of the dirtiest water. My name may be there, but…I wouldn't blame you for calling me an incompetent, if I go and do that…" Loren was not willing to read the signature that was alleged to be his.

Loren's investments were scrutinized. Arzo's attorney tried to show that the Pebble Beach Hotel was a waste of good money, because nobody stayed there. Loren's attorney established that the Pebble Beach Hotel had been built in the hopes that the railroad would build a station there; that explained any excessive expenses. It was learned that portions of his ranch were sold to the lighthouse department and to the Steele family. The rest was leased. Loren anticipated selling all but the Merced ranch for five million dollars; then he would leave Pescadero and invest money in United States bonds at four percent.

He was questioned about his association with a crook named Ragland and his building lots in Fresno. Loren constantly replied that he didn't know anything, that if he owed anybody money he would pay, and that if he made a mistake he would rectify it.

"Have you had him," Treat inquired, referring to Wally, "examined by physicians from time to time to see if anything could be done for him?"

"Not lately, but years ago I tried."

"And did they report to you whether or not his case was hopeless."

"They didn't see any show for him recovering."

On the twelfth day of the trial, Treat summarized Loren's personal, professional and legal history and told of the inconveniences caused by the painful trials.

"And in the event the court should decide you to be incompetent," said Treat to Coburn, "what do you understand the court will then do?"

"Well, take possession of all I have and set me out. If I wanted four bits I would have to ask other parties for four bits or a dollar for breakfast out of my own money. And I thought that wasn't exactly fair, as long as I worked all my lifetime for it."

Treat then asked some personal questions. He sought to prove that, aside from ordinary lapses in memory, his client could take care of himself physically. "Do you wake up during the night or do you sleep throughout the night?"

"I generally wake up about once a night…"

"Now with reference to your habits, Mr. Coburn, are you a man that drinks liquor, intoxicating liquor?"

"Very light on the liquor business and tobacco and such…"

Coburn refuted accusations that he tried to sell City Hall in San Francisco, or that he ever bribed any judges. Regarding wills, Loren said his intention had been to divide his property among all of his relatives, "but they couldn't wait that long, and so now I made up my mind that I should let somebody else have a little interest in it." His voice barely carried in the courtroom—then the octogenarian suddenly collapsed on the stand. Coburn was unable to continue, and Judge Dooling called a recess.

When the case resumed, Carl Coburn, in his ingratiating manner, said that he hoped he could do something for "dear Uncle Loren". He told the court he and Arzo visited a San Francisco attorney many years earlier to have an "equitable" will drawn up for Loren.

Equitable?

"Why," explained Carl, with a gleam in his eye, "a will that would be fair to all the relatives of the name of Coburn...including brothers and sisters and his sister-in-law Miss Upton."

In this ideal will all debts would be paid, with one hundred thousand dollars going to the Union Trust Company, made out in Wally's name, as an investment. Upon Wally's death, the remainder was to go to Arzo's wife, Lucy, to J.C.'s wife, and to Sarah. It gave the house and lot to Wally, and if he died first, it went to Lucy and Sarah; one-eighth share to J.C., Arzo, Alonzo, Lemuel, and Jesse Coburn (the latter three had died), as well as other relatives. The will, witnessed by Carl and Arzo, established Lucy Coburn and Sarah as Wally's guardian. J.C. was named the executor. It was what Loren wanted, said Carl.

When it was his turn, Arzo maintained that his interest in the trial was worth about fifteen thousand dollars. Treat tried to paint the sordid picture of a conspiracy masterminded by Arzo and Carl, but Matt Sullivan countered by introducing the damning deed to Sarah for four hundred acres, dated 1898. That deed was a weak link in Coburn's case, because he apparently did deed the land to Sarah, his sister-in-law at the time, but because he was paying the taxes he considered it to be his property.

Sarah testified that she was born in 1850 in Barrie, Vermont, but other birth records indicate that she was born in 1837. In court she took some thirteen years off her age, but Sarah looked all of her seventy-three years.

She described life at home: "...Mr. Coburn and his son Wallace enjoy the comforts of life...Wally has the freedom of the house and is not confined in any way. He eats at the table with the members of the family. He is permitted his own time with reference to eating."

"What care does he require?" interjected Judge Dooling.

"Well, not anything special, except to see that he dresses himself all right and to see that his food is all right…"

"Do you take him out for a ride in the carriage?"

Sarah shook her head and said "no."

"It is better to keep him at home, in a room?"

"Yes."

"Are the doors always left open?"

"Yes, so that he can go out at any time he wishes into the yard. It is a large yard. He walks out into it. I guess it is about fifty by one hundred feet…"

Sarah added that the "servant in the house was a Chinaman who had been in the household for seventeen years…He is very kind to Wally…" About Loren she said, "…As a matter of fact, Loren Coburn devoted his life to his agricultural business and livery business…"

Manual Goularte, the Pescadero blacksmith, testified that in his opinion, Loren had an unsound mind. He based his view on the fact that Loren constantly brought up the story about the deed from Mexico or Spain. He added that Loren sent out faulty bills and that he had been that way for the last four or five years.

J. Early Craig defended Loren's competency. He said that tenants refused to pay Loren the rent because of the hearings. Loren, he admitted, "…is a secretive man about matters that he doesn't think you have any business to know. He has always been reticent, in one instance, about commenting upon the exact condition of his son…" Craig said his father William, also an attorney, was on Loren's side during the Pigeon Point affair in the 1870's and against him during the Pebble Beach War, and then again with him during the 1899 incompetency hearing.

*San Francisco Call* reporter Harry Davids took the stand and was asked if he attributed Loren's embarrassment at his own wedding to the fact that he hadn't been in church for fifty years.

"No," said Davids. "I attributed it to the situation existing at the time of the wedding…It was presumed to be a secret, but the newspaper reporters were there in force…"

Judge Hebbard, who made a will out for Loren the day after the wedding, said, "…As I observed Mr. Coburn…so overcome at the awfulness, as it seems…of a proceeding to strip him of his control of the estate which it has taken him years to accumulate, there is a desperation about it and indignation which sends the blood quivering through these veins and makes him nervous and sometimes makes him so he cannot remember…And I have no doubt from Mr. Coburn's testimony that he just feels like getting up and hitting somebody…"

The proceedings wore Loren down, and it was reported that he fell from his new automobile in San Francisco, suffering abrasions. "…The landowner had been pleased at his trade of a string of blind horses for the car," ridiculed the *Examiner*, "but when he was hurt, he exclaimed: 'Well, I didn't get the best of the bargain, after all'…"

The trial, which covered two thousand five hundred pages, was moved to San Francisco for more testimony and the final arguments. H.B. Field, manager of the Yosemite House, the San Francisco rooming house where Loren and Sarah often stayed, took the stand. He described Loren's spending habits. Field said that now that he was married, Coburn paid one dollar for a double room; before he married Sarah the couple rented single rooms at seventy-five cents each. Sometimes Loren paid with a paper dollar, and at other times he gave the manager a gold piece and asked for change.

Lafayette Chandler, a wealthy Pescadero farmer, said that Loren was rational. The other half of Arzo's counsel, Theodore Roche, countered: "Haven't you repeatedly during the last five years told each of these gentlemen [pointing at witnesses Edward Gayety, Carl Coburn, and Manual Goularte] at Pescadero that Loren Coburn was crazy?"

"No, I don't think so," said Chandler.

"And ought to be hanged…Didn't you say substantially that—that the old man's mind was not in good condition?"

"I don't think so," deadpanned the farmer.

Treat nailed down Chandler's position regarding Carl Coburn: "Do you know Carl Coburn's reputation for truth and integrity discussed in the town of Pescadero."

"Well, it is pretty crooked sometimes I think…He is liable to be a little tricky and deceiving; don't stick to his word always from hearsay."

Mrs. Louise Woodham, a Pescadero resident, showed sympathy for Loren. She told the court of shenanigans with Loren's property: "…[Edward] Gayety said Mr. Coburn had deeded him ten thousand acres of land, and he only wished that it was good…" He had added cryptically "…We have got the old man now…"

When Loren talked to her, she said that he talked about the ranch "or some little local happening about town, the same as anybody would talk…" Mrs. Woodham identified with the old man's bitterness toward Gayety, "when I found what he was doing towards Mr. Coburn…He came to our house and said that these other Coburns would get that property very soon…"

M.J. Perry, Pescadero's lucid Justice-of-the-Peace, noted that Carl Coburn asked him to test Loren's competency by trying to lease the Catholic Church property from the old man. He got the lease on February 1, 1908. When asked for his opinion about Loren's mental condition, he said: "…He don't act like a man that is crazy, but he acts rather foolish in a good many respects…If you are talking of important matters to him, he will drift off on grants and running the government on sixty-cents on the dollar, and he will say he carried on a lawsuit for eleven years…I told him I was going to testify against him; I was going to testify that he was not competent, but I said it is to help you, and the old man got laughing actually…I told him he didn't have to pay his debts if they declared him incompetent, and he laughed. He actually believes if you would declare him incompetent, he wouldn't have to pay his debts at all. He said it was for these parties to prove the land across the creek wasn't his. The leasing of the church property was not a trick; it was simply testing him—whether the old man could be influenced to do something wrong, that perhaps would injure him…Some rascal from the outside might get in there and get fairly intimate with him and he could influence him to do anything…"

The witnesses came and went.

San Francisco attorney Crittenden Thornton, who had practiced law for forty-one years, said he'd known Loren since 1858, when he owned the stable in San Francisco, and that his father had represented Loren in those days.

"Loren," he said,"…was exceedingly fond of litigation…I had five cases for him which included the case of Coburn against [George] Hearst [the mining millionaire], which was compromised for five thousand dollars…" Coburn was often successful in litigation, especially under John Thornton. "…The way he [ his father, John] got to be Coburn's attorney," said the younger Thornton, "he was the plaintiff's attorney in the action of Steele against Coburn and Clark, and beat Coburn out of his boots…"

A.J. Jarman, a young San Francisco businessman, took the stand. "Did you ever have any conversation with Loren Coburn about the report that his tenants were stealing grain from him?" asked A.J. Treat.

"I told him that the rumor had come to me from a very reliable source that certain of his tenants were stealing from him. He said that probably was so, but he says on the whole he got about what he was fairly entitled to…"

"Did he ever say anything to you about having trusted Carl Coburn?"

"He started in about the sudden sadness of the death of his wife," said Jarman, as he related the old man's tragedies, "and about his son, and he said that his son was not able to participate in the affairs of life, as referring to me, as I was; and he said he would have given most all his property if he had had a son like myself to help him, and he spoke about his son not being able to help him—he said he was helpless, and he said he had to turn to someone and he attempted to turn to Carl. He says he is not a Coburn at all; he says he is somebody else, and he says I wanted to treat him as a son and he abused my confidence, and he says now, I have got no one…"

Jarman testified that Loren said "…he had a great deal of sadness in his life, and that he had started as a poor man and worked up, and his wife was very devoted to him…and said that this illness, or this unfortunate condition of his son was a great sadness in their lives; that they could not enjoy the company of other people as other people do at their homes, and his wife's life was very sad for that reason, because she couldn't go out and mingle among other people as she would like to, and he said that she had died and that he had no one that thought anything of him, or did anything for him, excepting Miss Upton..."

When he visited Loren at the Hotel Yosemite, Jarman was shocked to see the wealthy man living in such meager surroundings. "...I said to him, 'Mr. Coburn, a man of your wealth should not put up at a little place like this; this is a frame building and nothing but wooden partitions, and it is a little drafty in here, and you haven't all the comforts of life, and a man of your age should be at a better hotel. I says you can afford it, and I says I stop at the St. Francis and I haven't any part of your wealth and you are stopping over here'...

"Well, I have been accustomed to this place for a great number of years during my life," Jarman said that Coburn told him, "and I would feel a little out of place in those high-toned places, and he says it is more economical. I have everything I desire."

Jarman's words made an impact on the courtroom.

Theodore Roche, Arzo's counsel, waived the privilege of making an opening statement and said he would be content with a rebuttal of the testimony. Archibald Treat contended that his client conducted business affairs as efficiently as he had fifty years earlier. He argued that the accumulation of the fortune proved that Loren was very competent, indeed.

This would not end the trials involving Loren Coburn. Loren was determined to regain his competency. He had worked all his life to collect the land he owned; he was not about to let it go to the conniving relatives whom he despised so much. As he became embittered, the thirst for revenge matched the singlemindedness of owning land that once dominated his life.

# CARL MAKES TROUBLE

Gossip held that Carl Coburn had lost the job of County Supervisor three years earlier to Dr. Daniel Blackburn because he was disloyal to his constituency. Then in 1910 Dr. Blackburn, whom Carl hated, was reelected to another four-year term; the people showed confidence in the handsome dentist. However, Carl, believing in his own powers of persuasion, actually thought that he could turn the people against Blackburn; he didn't think it would "bounce back on him like a rubber ball". And so he was responsible for a scandal that exposed Dr. Blackburn to criminal allegations of bribery.

The scandal came to light in the screaming headlines of the *San Francisco Examiner*. Four indictments were brought down by the Goldman Grand Jury against current and former officials of San Mateo County. It was a timely topic; San Francisco had cleaned house, purging its own mayor and others. The newspaper began the sensational expose in a series of articles that reported the confessions of three men who described the methods by which members of the Board of Supervisors favored the H.S. Crocker Company for furniture bids for the courthouse. Bribes were paid by Charles Marshall, an agent for Crocker, and Jesse Marks, the "go-between".

Carl Coburn, the former Supervisor, helped by turning informer. He invited government officials to overhear a conversation he had with Supervisor Blackburn in his own store in Pescadero. Also present, but unseen, were *Examiner* reporters and Assistant Attorney General Benjamin. Holes had been bored into a wall behind Carl's office so that the observers could hear Supervisor Blackburn incriminate himself. The Supervisor was tricked into talking about election money he received, and he detailed how bribes were paid for prizefight permits. He also disclosed a plan to establish a roadhouse and open a gambling house and develop other deals that were underway. "There'll be about five hundred dollars apiece in the furniture deal," Blackburn told Carl.

A few days earlier an *Examiner* reporter had watched Supervisor Blackburn enter Carl's store and make out a check payable to C.J. Coburn for four hundred and twenty-six dollars. It was endorsed on the reverse side "payable on or after December 15, 1910. D.E. Blackburn." As evidence of wrongdoing, the check was turned over to Assistant Attorney General Benjamin. At that time, Carl gave the attorney his story about graft in San Mateo County.

The bribery ring fell apart as Marks, the "go-between" revealed to the authorities that six thousand dollars left at his cigar store was to be split five ways. Marks said that Marshall, the Crocker furniture agent, told him there would be twenty-five percent of the contract price of the furniture for the Supervisors. Marshall admitted that the money was to be passed to the Supervisors; he corroborated Carl's statements.

The Attorney General's office and the D.A. initiated legal action. The San Francisco Grand Jury was summoned to investigate the bribery of San Mateo County officials by the H.S. Crocker Company.

Amazingly, witness Carl Coburn revealed that he himself had accepted a bribe. Carl testified that he became acquainted with Charles Marshall in Redwood City, where he discussed buying furniture for the courthouse. Marshall dealt directly with the Supervisors and was acquainted with all of its members.

"…The furniture contract," said Carl, "was for twenty-five thousand dollars, and Marshall was the agent for the Crocker Company. The Art Metal Company was competing with the Crocker Company, and its bid was for twenty thousand dollars against the Crocker's company bid of twenty-five thousand dollars.

"The Supervisors, however, expressed the opinion that the Crocker Company furniture would be better than the Art Metal Company's furniture—that is, all of them with the exception of Supervisor McBain.

"The Crocker Company finally got the contract," continued Carl. "The contract was signed two or three weeks after it was awarded, and the furniture was delivered...

"This contract was awarded to the Crocker Company prior to the earthquake of 1906, which destroyed the courthouse. Efforts were made to have the contract made void in the period pending the reconstruction of the courthouse, and Bullock, the D.A. was asked to write the Crocker Company about the matter. The whole thing, in fact, was left in Bullock's hands."

Not until 1910, during the Coburn guardianship proceedings, did Carl see Marshall again, and by then he had not been the County Supervisor for three years, thereby absolving himself of any guilt in what happened afterward.

Superior Judge George Buck instructed the Grand Jury to probe graft in the County. After an all-night session where six hours of testimony were heard, the Grand Jury returned with indictments for conspiracy to extort against Dr. Blackburn for agreeing to accept a bribe. He was arrested at his Pescadero home and ordered to stand trial.

While Carl may have put a blot on Dr. Blackburn's reputation, he too was indicted for conspiracy to extort. Perhaps the feeling of wrongdoing was not uncomfortable for Carl Coburn. To the villagers he was exposed as an informer.

# JUDGE DOOLING'S DECISION

Before Judge Maurice Dooling's decision was rendered in August of 1910, Loren took the stand and made a speech. He insisted that he was physically and mentally fit and able to manage his own affairs. He concluded by saying that if he were incompetent then so was the court and everybody else.

Those in the courtroom strained to hear as Judge Dooling spoke. "In the case at bar," he began, "the respondent cannot be held insane," he said, disagreeing with Dr. Lustig's assessment that Loren suffered from senile dementia. "But he is mentally incompetent to manage his property as a result of weakness of mind and memory arising from old age."

*Loren was found incompetent a second time.*

The fact that Coburn remembered so few of the leases that he signed and that he regarded the four hundred acres he deeded to his wife as his own were believed to support the Judge's decision that the landowner was incompetent. This time he appointed San Francisco Public Administrator M.J. Hynes as the guardian of Loren's person and his property.

Archibald Treat, the chief counsel for Loren, asked for a rehearing in the matter. He based his plea on the statement that the witness Carl Coburn was a "man of bad character". Treat backed up his attack with the contention that Carl conspired to kill Loren and Sarah by offering two ranchers five thousand dollars cash to "get rid of them" so that he might acquire the estate. The attorney read an affidavit signed by four Pescadero residents charging Carl with a lack of personal integrity. The affidavits documented the courthouse-furniture scandal in which Carl confessed to taking a bribe of three hundred and forty dollars after he involved Supervisor Blackburn and others.

But, amazingly, the court did not take the statements seriously, and it declared that Loren was likely to be imposed upon or deceived by artful or designing persons.

During the hearing, seven hundred and fifty thousand words of evidence, together with voluminous briefs, were entered into the record.

The newspapers called the case a remarkable one and commented on Loren's method of getting rich. It was said that he bought land but seldom sold any. "...To carry out this policy, he has engaged in hundreds of lawsuits and pitched battles."

True to his nature, Loren had not lost his fighting spirit. He would try to control as much of his estate as possible. He asked his lawyers to get an order restraining Hynes as a guardian.

But while the decision was being appealed, Loren leased much of his valuable land to a stranger.

# PART V

## THE NEWCOMERS

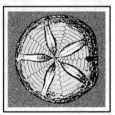

# CHAPTER THIRTY

# CHRIS WIDEMANN COMES TO TOWN

In 1912 Loren Coburn's name appeared for the hundredth time in San Mateo County Superior Court records. Henry W. Walker was suing him for an unpaid stenographer's bill amounting to $184.35. Walker complained that he had received only one hundred dollars out of a $284.35 bill. Another court reporter was suing Loren for $824, an amount he said was due for services rendered in Judge Dooling's court two years earlier.

Loren was suing Robert Reece to recover $1,986.46, which he said was his share of farm products sold by the defendant.

Christian ("Chris") H. Widemann was a new name that began to appear in the court records. The thirty-five-year-old, one of the most colorful men in the Salinas Valley, was Loren's most enterprising tenant on the ten-thousand-acre King City ranch. They had known each other for several years. Widemann was born in the area, a grandson of successful general store owners. From an early age Chris preferred the best things in life, and when he had the money he was generous. As a young man he owned a string of race horses; he also worked in the family store and became the vice president of the Bank of Gonzales.

A bachelor, Widemann was a clean shaven, stout man who looked elegant in coat and tie, accessorized with a diamond stick pin and cuff links. This important man was suddenly seen in Pescadero frequently.

It was Widemann who was named in a law suit asking for rent against a Coastside farmer named Sherpa, for $2,870 interest and $750 for attorney's fees. Sherpa had leased the "Little Butano" ranch from Loren.

How did Widemann, who hailed from Monterey county, get involved with Loren in Pescadero?

Loren had sold his Gazos Creek timber interests to Widemann. After Loren was judged incompetent in Dooling's court, Widemann leased nearly all of Loren's land. With Carl and Arzo finagling to take control of his estate, Loren turned to Widemann. With his breezy confidence boosted by having grown-up wealthy, Widemann convinced Loren that his management style would relieve him of all his burdens and the need for a guardian, and it would "put those money-hungry relatives to shame".

Eager to accumulate great wealth but lacking restraint and fiscal responsibility, Widemann had grandiose plans. He intended to build eight miles of railroad track and to construct a lumber mill. Widemann purchased all the timber bark and wood on four thousand acres of Loren's land. The impressive work of the Southern Pacific Railroad in Monterey County, including the luxurious Hotel Del Monte, had inspired him. At Pigeon Point, which he modernized, Widemann started a goat-milk ranch; he also brought five hundred sheep to Pescadero. But there was more that he was going to do, and Loren handed over lease after lease.

Cutting in his partner, the older Ed Eaton, Widemann was going to install a planing mill at Pigeon Point, capable of handling all of their lumber from the Gazos. A general merchandise store and a warehouse with holding capacity of two thousand tons of hay was to be built and a ten-ton scale installed. In preparation for the steamers expected to call, a party of divers was hired to settle anchors and attach buoys—all of this at Pigeon Point.

To secure the loyalty of the villagers, Widemann set up an office, announcing that he would buy hay, grain, and produce, and pay cash on the spot. Best of all, he provided local employment.

Things were looking up. Scores of auto parties stopped at the Pebble Beach Hotel. An auto stage delivered passengers from Santa Cruz to Pescadero in three hours, a trip that formerly took all day.

With Widemann came an entourage that grew with time. Ed Eaton, his wife, Fanny, son, and daughter moved into the Pebble Beach Hotel until their home in the village was completed. Ed was friendly and very likable. On the Fourth of July when the village band played and the

Native Daughter's float was drawn by four black horses, Eaton jokingly offered a prize of five dollars to all the ladies over forty-five who would run in a race, winner to take all. He wasn't surprised to discover that there were no ladies over forty-five in Pescadero, and thus there was no race.

Andy Stirling, a former deputy sheriff, followed his boss to Pescadero, as did Widemann's "secretary", the attractive and well-dressed Josephine Vosti. John Clements, a black man who worked as a chauffeur, came as well. Others joined the charismatic Widemann in the months to come. The men lived together in a rented house.

With Widemann on the scene, a number of changes occurred. Loren's big land holdings were divided into smaller parcels and leased to tenants for a number of years instead of annually. Future plans included construction of comfortable ranch houses intended to attract a better class of tenants. About one hundred Japanese people moved into the vicinity and cultivated beans on what used to be called the Coburn ranch but was now called "Widemann's ranch".

By this time the old, drinking brother-in-law, Marraton Upton had died at age eighty-four. The Coburn household had thinned out with only Loren, Sarah, Wally, and Ah Gee living there.

A close relationship developed between Loren and Widemann. Frequently, Widemann, who collected expensive, flashy automobiles, drove with Loren and Sarah to San Francisco.

Some people viewed Widemann's management style as a good business move for Loren, who now received rent in cash semi-annually; there were no crops to divide, and he did not have to hire anyone to get checks for the rental of his property.

Loren gloated over the sale of the timber and the leasing of his ranches. He thought he was a better manager than any guardian, although a number of people owed him money. He told his debtors that now was a good time to settle accounts.

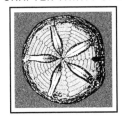

# CHAPTER THIRTY-ONE

# THE THIRD COMPETENCY TRIAL – 1913

*"Coburn is probably the most notorious litigant in the state, having carried on over one thousand cases in the courts in the last fifty years."*
—*New York Tribune*

Loren looked after the details of a new hearing in his competency case. Luck was not on his side. The Appellate Court acceded to the State Supreme Court's command to review the case, but Judge Dooling's decision was not reversed, and the incompetency judgment held. Archibald Treat appealed to the U.S. Supreme Court, but it refused to review the case.

Meanwhile the gossip in Pescadero was that Loren was buying new furniture and a new auto, actions seemingly out of character.

His nephew Arzo and his wife Lucy were living in a rented, one-story frame house in Pescadero. It stood next door to the house rented for Widemann's men. But there were reports that Arzo was going to "build a nice large house", which meant that he intended to stay a long time, waiting for an inheritance from his wealthy Uncle Loren. Perhaps the trolley company he owned had fallen on hard times. He decided to visit his Uncle's King City ranch property where Chris Widemann managed the ten thousand acres.

Despite Loren's attempt to limit the power of his court-appointed guardian, M.J. Hynes proceeded as his legal estate manager. But Loren stubbornly refused to acknowledge Hynes—who was authorized to collect rents and to buy and sell land and equipment. To get the accounting records, Hynes had to arm himself with a court order, and with Arzo he marched to Loren's house. They were rebuked, forcing Hynes to call for the Justice-of-the-Peace and the Constable to legally take Loren's books away from him.

Loren ordered his attorney to do anything in his power to restore his rights before he lost all his land.

There was reason to doubt Hynes's abilities. He could not leave the estate alone: he wanted to lease the two ten thousand acre ranches at once; he wanted to sell uncut timber and to compromise lawsuits brought by Widemann. The Widemann contracts were made when Loren's competency case was before the State Supreme Court, and there was a legal question as to the validity of those leases. Hynes's decisions were not those Loren would have made.

But Judge Buck granted Hynes the authority to lease or sell the ranches at King City and Pescadero. Hynes rewrote the agreement with Widemann to lease the King City ranch for ten years, with an option to buy after five years for three hundred and twenty-six thousand dollars. Widemann was to pay an annual rent of twenty thousand dollars for five years and then ten thousand dollars annually for the lifetime of the lease.

Loren's unwanted guardian sold adjoining King City tracts to the Spreckles Sugar Company for ninety-nine thousand dollars. This land was supposedly sold to raise funds to develop the property at Pescadero.

The San Mateo newspapers complained bitterly that San Mateo County was losing revenue—the guardian should have been appointed from San Mateo and not San Francisco, they said, so that the attorney's fees would be left in the local coffers.

Attorney Treat filed an action against Hynes in San Mateo County Superior Court; if he could win, Loren's competency would be restored. Now eighty-seven, Coburn looked forward to a jury trial in the fall of 1913. It would be a battle between Coburn and M.J. Hynes. He hired a battery of lawyers including Archibald Treat, Percy Henshall, Albert Mansfield, and John McNab. Hynes was represented by Matt Sullivan and Thomas Hickey.

It was said to be the longest jury trial in San Mateo County and the most important and famous incompetency case tried for many years in California.

This time Arzo and Carl were not present in Judge George Cabaniss's courtroom in Redwood City. But Dr. Lustig, the "psychiatrist", was in constant attendance, jotting down notes about Loren's behavior.

Loren felt vigorous. He showed a strong mental state on the stand, but on cross-examination he could not remember the names of his attorneys or the judge's name. On the other hand he was knowledgeable about the small details regarding Widemann's lease. Percy Henshall pointed to contracts drawn up by Loren that proved the old man could manage his own affairs.

Reporter Michael Williams was impressed with Loren's conduct in court. He wrote: "With all due deference to the various judges and juries that have considered Loren Coburn unfit to manage his own affairs, this reporter must still testify that he personally found the ancient gentleman as lively and as sound in his intellectuals as he seems to be in his wind, his limbs, and his senses five."

A major witness for the defense was Judge George Buck who testified as to why he had declared Loren incompetent: it was, he said, because the old man's mind had failed him, and he signed deeds to property that he didn't own when the papers were presented to him by people in whom he had no confidence.

Still Loren believed that he would be declared competent. "Although I have earned more than one million dollars in the eighty-seven years of my existence," he said, "I will consider my life a failure unless the jury before Judge George Cabaniss in Redwood City declares that I am competent." Coburn claimed it cost him one hundred thousand dollars to defend himself from the money-grubbing relatives.

The jurors wept in the last hours of Loren's case. Speaking for one-hour and twenty-six minutes, John L. McNab painted a sympathetic picture of his client: "This poor old man stands before you, a pathetic figure, his face freighted with the pathos of the years. The verdict to be rendered this day marks the final milestone in the life of Loren Coburn. If it shall be against him he will turn his face to the sunset, and hopelessness will be his portion to the end of his days. There in his lonely home in Pescadero he can throw his arms around his imbecile boy and weep out his helplessness and his hopelessness. With his poor white-haired wife and helpless son he stands in pathetic silence awaiting your judgment. If your verdict still be against him, he will drown a cry that will be better than death."

Matt Sullivan said that Coburn had been declared incompetent by two Superior Court Judges and that the State Supreme Court was not the proper custodian of his holdings. Therefore his competency should not be restored, he argued. The final outcome of the case was in the hands of the twelve jurors, all of them men.

The jury could not agree, and *the case was dismissed.*

Eight jurors were in favor and four against; one more vote, and he would have won. Louis J. Flanders, the jury foreman, who voted for Loren, said that the four votes against him were due to Judge Buck's testimony. Buck's appearance in his own courtroom as a witness was considered unusual, and it damaged Coburn's defense.

Coburn applied for a new jury trial. He said he would go on fighting until he had exhausted every means and all of his money.

The case was transferred to San Francisco, where the jurors were not as familiar with Loren's many legal battles.

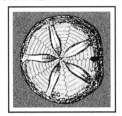

# CHAPTER THIRTY-TWO

# LOREN WINS ONE – 1914

A year later at the new jury trial in San Francisco, Loren felt feisty. The same groups of lawyers were retained by Coburn and Hynes as had represented the litigants at the 1913 jury trial. Judge Cabaniss presided again.

On opening day, just as in the early days, the courtroom was packed with spectators. There was the familiar parade of witnesses. Loren's business associates and acquaintances vouched for his sanity. But J.Early Craig rocked the courtroom with a new revelation. On one occasion, he divulged, Arzo tried to pass off a disguised Carl as one D.V. Delmas—but Loren was too clever to be fooled. Prior to the 1910 proceedings, Arzo came to his office and offered to drop the lawsuit against his uncle if Loren paid him fifteen thousand dollars for previous legal fees, an additional forty thousand dollars, and the guarantee that all the blood relatives would be included in the will. Judge Cabaniss said that the facts were relevant to a will contest, but there was no place for them at this hearing. Still, the words had been heard by the jury.

A relaxed Ed Eaton, Widemann's business partner, took the stand and said that Loren was rational, but on cross-examination Matt Sullivan accused Eaton of corrupt practices. Sullivan got Eaton to admit that Loren trusted his and Widemann's every word, down to every bushel of grain shipped and sold, and that it blinded Loren to the devious things going on. Sullivan charged that Eaton and Widemann reported selling Loren's timber at less than market value, and taxes that they agreed to pay were included in a bill sent to Loren.

Confident, but reserved, Widemann testified that Loren possessed good business judgment. Sarah took the stand and confirmed that her husband was rational.

Although he showed lapses in memory, Loren was a bright witness. After sixty-three years of hard work, he said that all he wanted to do was to retire, and that was why he turned the business over to Widemann and Eaton.

M.J. Hynes's defense was built on the foundation that Loren benefited from his guardianship. This was toppled by Treat's sharp criticism that Hynes left Loren's estate worse off than it was before.

The trial ended on Friday the 13th of March in 1914. Hynes's attorneys argued that Widemann and Eaton were not the kind benefactors they portended to be; instead they were opportunists who saw Loren as an easy mark. They were the ones Loren should be wary of; they were the ones tricking him into disastrous contracts. That description was not lost on the jury. Treat's plea to the jury was to "Let the old man live out his last days in peace".

Judge Buck had asked the jurors if they harbored any superstitions about Friday the 13th; no one did. It was a lucky day for Loren Coburn.

The jurors returned quickly with a verdict: The *"pioneer capitalist" was restored to competency.*

"This verdict gives me new life," exclaimed the old man. "I feel spry as if I was only forty years old." Loren promised to erect a pretty house in Pescadero and to live out his life in comfort.

The Arzo Coburns returned to the East Coast.

It was said that Loren's rights were restored because Hynes was tired of taking care of the mixed-up estate and because strong testimony against Coburn was omitted.

John McNab, one of Loren's attorneys, remarked that if Loren had not been so wealthy, no one would have bothered about his guardianship.

Now that Loren was finally in control of his life again, M.J. Hynes was obliged to file a final accounting of the estate. It covered seventy-eight pages and left a one hundred and sixty thousand dollars balance or net gain. This pleased Loren, but he forgot that a great part of his land holdings had been sold. Hynes also presented Loren with a bill for thirty thousand dollars to cover his services and his lawyer's fees. Loren didn't object to paying this, but he did object to Treat's bill for seventy-five thousand dollars, covering six years of legal work. Henshall billed Loren for seventeen thousand dollars and McNab for thirty thousand dollars.

*Loren refused to pay them all.*

Soon after the trial Loren was in San Francisco, where he signed new contracts with Chris Widemann for the lease of his Pescadero ranch, for the sale of his timber, and for the use of his landing at Pigeon Point. It was said the deal should make him two hundred thousand dollars richer.

All the lawyers who helped Loren regain his competency sued him for nonpayment of legal fees. Indefatigable, Loren hired his old adversaries Matt Sullivan and Eustace Cullinan to defend him against "them parasite lawyers". In a wise move, Sullivan and Cullinan got a retaining fee first and a contract for services rendered. The jury granted Treat fifty thousand dollars.

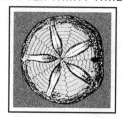

# CHAPTER THIRTY-THREE

# CARL MAKES TROUBLE AGAIN

Chris Widemann and Ed Eaton were respected because they provided good jobs for the isolated community. Considered a "nice man", Widemann was famous for his barbecues—featuring duck, quail, doves, and venison. He wore snappy suits, owned expensive cars driven by chauffeurs, and spent a great deal of his time in San Francisco. The fancy cars, distinguished by their flat hoods, unusual at the time, caused heads to turn in Pescadero.

The villagers called it "Widemann's Reign", and his underlings who "took care of things" were dubbed "Widemann's stooges", and together they were known as "the Widemann Family".

Well known in Monterey County, Widemann was now the big man in Pescadero. That meant a vested interest in politics, and he supported the candidacy of Dr. Clarence Victor (C.V.) Thompson for County Supervisor. Dr. Thompson challenged Dr. Blackburn. Results of the election leaned in Thompson's direction by a narrow margin; now his friendship with Widemann deepened—the village Supervisor/physician and the landowner.

According to the 1915 *Salinas Valley Rustler's* "Colonists and Homeseeker's Edition", there was a place called Coburn located between King City and Soledad in Monterey. Coburn was located on Loren's property, of course; it was the place he had named after himself, but the real estate article said that the land was subdivided and irrigated by Widemann.

Thirty years earlier Loren owned a large portion of the San Lorenzo Rancho, extending all the way north to the Cholame creek and the

Greenfield crossing. Three years later he deeded land to the Southern Pacific, a customary practice when trying to entice the railroad to put a station on one's property. The SP announced plans for completing their coastal line linking San Francisco with Los Angeles. The rights-of-way and easements had been donated and bought in the Salinas Valley—but a different route was chosen and Loren was left out.

Yet in 1915 the place called Coburn was "fast becoming the comfortable home of a colony of prosperous dairymen, as a number of buildings have already been erected..." Supposedly the tract had been sold out in eight months. It sounded similar to what Widemann had planned for "the New Pescadero".

Questions of intrigue refused to leave the Loren Coburns alone. Now it was Mr. Guggenheim—a representative of Eastern financial interests, who said that he had purchased the ailing Ocean Shore Railroad—who approached Loren about selling his ranch. Guggenheim bragged about the railroad's big plans and asked for Loren's selling price. Loren answered twelve million dollars.

This ridiculous price did not stop the men from haggling; Guggenheim finally agreed to buy for ten million dollars. A contract was signed with Sarah as the witness. Guggenheim turned over a check for five million dollars and a note at eight percent interest. Then he left town. The details were to be worked out when Guggenheim returned, but he never did return.

The San Mateo County newspapers carried shocking news that Sarah had filed an incompetency petition, asking that she be assigned her husband's legal guardian. One story circulated that Loren's lawyers advised Sarah to do this to keep "the thieving nephews" away, but it turned out to be false. Another story claimed that someone named Harry Blas persuaded Sarah to file the motion.

Mysterious people came and went, and some of them were faceless, but the target was Sarah.

A furious Ed Eaton, Widemann's normally sedate partner, waved the San Francisco and San Mateo newspapers in Loren's face. He was incensed that one "James Sexton" of Los Angeles and New York filed an agreement in the County Recorder's office for the sale of the entire ten thousand-acre Pescadero ranch for one hundred thousand dollars. This document was witnessed by a "Thomas Blake". Sexton paid fifteen thousand dolllars down, was given all of the crops grown that year, and had full power to collect rents.

Loren told Eaton it was "a fraud"; he and Sarah drove to San Francisco to consult with lawyers.

Later the couple appeared in Superior Court to testify in their lawsuit against the "mysterious James Sexton". Their purpose was to squelch the deed, but Sexton never appeared.

Yet another unexplained document surfaced. This was a notarized deal between Sarah and Paul Guggenheim, the man who said he represented Eastern railroad interests. Guggenheim was to pay Sarah fifty thousand dollars to get her husband to sign an agreement selling the Pescadero property for one hundred thousand dollars.

Interestingly, Carl Coburn colored in the background of this document. He said Guggenheim came to his store asking for his wife, Minnie, a notary. She accompanied him to Loren's house to notarize the controversial document.

Carl said that this proved Sarah was scheming to get part of Loren's estate. Finally, Carl produced another document, this a will made by Loren with Sarah as his sole beneficiary. It gave her power-of-attorney.

Most people thought it curious that Carl Coburn was the only one who had all these documents.

To clear her name, Sarah hired Eustace Cullinan to track down Guggenheim, Sexton, and Blake. It came as no surprise that they didn't exist, but one man — a detective hired to deceive Loren — was acting as all three.

Cullinan's investigation led him to conclude that the plan was to make Sarah appear as "the designing person", enabling Carl and Arzo to press for a new incompetency suit. This was helped along by the fact that the villagers noticed Loren occasionally became so disoriented about his whereabouts that he had to ask where the road to Santa Cruz was—a direction any child would know.

Calling Arzo and Carl into his office, Cullinan made the pair sign a paper promising to turn over all of the incriminating documents. A dozen documents were found that had been typed on Carl's typewriter, including a power-of-attorney from Loren to Arzo and a consent to have a guardian appointed. There were documents with forged signatures and authentic signatures. It was said that the documents were switched before being signed. Carl learned to duplicate Loren's signature better than the old man could sign it himself.

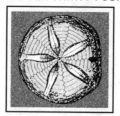

# CHAPTER THIRTY-FOUR

# A FARMING COUNTRYSIDE

The Ocean Shore Railroad courted bankruptcy and was unable to compete with the trucks that provided farmers with faster and more reliable service to market in San Francisco. It did not lay tracks farther south than Tunitas Creek, which was north of Pescadero and which left the village in the middle of nowhere.

Now an automobile-stage ferried passengers to Pescadero and to Santa Cruz, where train connections for Southern California could be made. The building of the Coastside Boulevard, a "high-class road" branching out to other communities and to San Francisco, quickly became a favorite road for Sunday afternoons.

The seven-passenger Red Star Stage serviced San Francisco, Half Moon Bay, and Pescadero; round-trip fare was four dollars. Pescadero, with a population of some one thousand, was publicized as a holiday resort easily accessible from the city.

At heart, though, Pescadero was really farming country. The lowlands and the foothills, conquered by Knapp's side-hill plow, were carpeted with vegetables. The artichoke—the "dainty aristocrat" among vegetables—developed a flavor attained no where else. Truck gardening was profitable. The best land rented for about five hundred dollars an acre, although it was said that three times that amount was not unusual for the most productive farms.

The 1910 United States census showed that the total value of all farm property in San Mateo County was worth over 20 million dollars, and most of it was located on the Coastside.

A little known fact was that millions of feet of untouched redwood lumber, the largest forest south of Mendocino county, lay along Pescadero creek and Butano and Gazos creeks to the south. In the Gazos, lumber operations actively turned timber into shingles and railroad ties. Widemann ran some of the operations.

A new industry was developed when Loren's ranch was converted into "one of the biggest goat ranches in the U.S." Chris Widemann imported five hundred milk goats from Mexico and lower California; the plan was to condense the milk and sell it for invalids and babies. The goats were fed alfalfa and milked by machine. A goatmilk cannery was built at Pigeon Point, near the condensary, and the employees walked the goat milk to the cannery. George Davis, a young boy, drove his father's Model T automobile to pick up the goat milk.

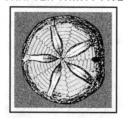

# CHAPTER THIRTY-FIVE

# WIDEMANN AND HIS FRIENDS

Chris Widemann rented another house east of town; this one was more impressive than the frame house occupied by his men; it was set back from the road and secluded in the trees. Called "the Social Club", Widemann lived there with the young, pretty Josephine "Josie" Vosti.

Widemann continued hosting lavish barbecues; he might invite his good friend, Gus Lapierre, a French chef who owned a restaurant in Salinas, to cook. Lapierre was experienced at preparing mallard duck, quail, and frogs' legs. But it was not just the delicious food and fine wines that drew people to "the Social Club"; gambling and pool tables were available to the guests.

The people who frequented "the Social Club" were not the ordinary citizens of Pescadero, but luminaries like Dr. C.V. Thompson, now the Chairman of the Board of Supervisors. Dr. Thompson visited his benefactor, Widemann, as did others; the Club was often full of revelers.

As a Supervisor and a doctor, Thompson's role was expansive: political regarding jobs and licenses, fatherly when it came to domestic issues. He was the man the villagers consulted about everyday problems; he was the man who could solve them. For example, before Valentine's Day in 1916 Sybil Easterday, the Coastside's eccentric sculptress, sent word that Dr. Thompson should come immediately to her home; her "husband", Louis Paulsen had been drinking heavily, and he threatened to do her bodily harm if she disturbed him. It was known that when drunk, Paulsen surrounded himself with an arsenal of firearms and barricaded himself in the back room of the saloon he ran at Tunitas Creek.

Dr. Thompson came at once with the Pescadero blacksmith, a known scrapper who had testified against Loren Coburn. The men broke down the locked doors and found Paulsen sitting dead in a chair, a wound in his chest. A double-barreled shotgun lay on the floor beside him. The death was ruled a suicide, but there were those who thought otherwise.

When in the mood to have a party with the Pacific Ocean as a backdrop, Widemann invited everyone to a bash at the Pebble Beach Hotel. His was the good life that Loren had missed.

For the villagers, Widemann arranged lively Christmas parties and bought gifts for all the children; he always showed his best manners with the Pescaderans. Like Thompson, Widemann had excellent political connections, which he used to ensure loyalty from the villagers. He helped locals who did not want to go to the Front in WWI.

Frequently he cooked dinner and drank liquor with Eaton, Stirling, and Clements at the rented house in the village.

The brown-haired Josie worked for Widemann as bookkeeper, secretary, and receptionist in the commissary, near the Emporium, the small store owned by Carl Coburn. There was not much business at Carl's store, however; the people distrusted him, and he was leaving town more often to cash checks to tide him over. Some of these checks turned out to be bad checks.

Through the commissary, Widemann would buy goods wholesale to supply his ranching and dairying needs, bypassing J.C. Williamson's general store. Bills were also paid there. "You had to go through Josie in Chris's office by the fire station to see him," said the locals.

Josie drove sporty cars, and the villagers remarked that "she didn't look like the type who worked". But sometimes she worked at the telephone company, which gave her an opportunity to screen calls.

The couple had known each other in King City, where she had also worked for Widemann and was said to be his mistress; they had lived together off and on for eight years.

The husky Widemann, who was older, stood six-feet tall and had an unshakable reputation as a womanizer. Josie begged him to settle down; she wanted to get married. Both were jealous, with fiery tempers, especially if Widemann saw Josie dancing with anyone else at the tiny IDES Hall in Pescadero.

Josie was known to have "a good arm for throwing things". There was a story that Widemann once sent Josie, who was ill, to his doctor in Salinas. The doctor told her that she needed an operation which Widemann would pay for; apparently Josie was pregnant. When it was over, she discovered to her horror that she could no longer have children. In anger she fled, as she often did in her sports car, to her rented room at 704 Bush Street in San Francisco. Predictably, she returned when she began to miss the good life that Widemann provided.

Together they often stayed at the Turpin Hotel on Powell Street in San Francisco—a romantic spot where the cable cars turned around. Josie was always with Widemann.

Other men from Widemann's past began turning up in Pescadero. One was Harry Zealand, whose business card read that he was the manager of the Union Launch Company at 52 Turk Street in San Francisco. Zealand occasionally worked as Widemann's chauffeur, as did Jockey Baker and John Clements, the black auto mechanic who was already in the village. Another outsider was J.F. Gooding, who also drove for Widemann; people marveled at Gooding's driving skills. They had never seen anyone park a car like he did, and common belief was that he was once a cab driver.

The former sailor and small-time pugilist Frank "Kid Zug", joined Widemann's gang. The 135-pound lightweight, who probably got his early training in violence in the back rooms of saloons, said he was a house painter from San Francisco, but he was never seen with a paint brush, although he was paid regularly by Widemann.

His presence led to the building of an outdoor prize-fighting ring at the south end of San Gregorio Street, not far from the village's landmark flagpole. At sixty, Kid Zug's boxing skills were only a shadow of what they had been thirty-five years earlier, but for the boys in town, the world champion Abe Attell could not have brought them more excitement.

Some of the time he lived at the dilapidated Swanton House, now a boarding house. He was always drunk; consequently nobody believed much of what he said. He had plenty of places to find liquor; *there were four saloons in the tiny village.*

Repeated beatings had left the small-time slugger with slurred speech and an often comic demeanor. People said he was "a little wacky from getting hit in the head". Yet his scarred face gave him the power to intimidate.

The most memorable bout in Pescadero's boxing history took place when Kid Zug was challenged by Happy Frey. Happy, son of the lady bartender at the Elkhorn Saloon and the village constable, was in his late twenties at the time. Kid Zug was sixty, and Happy predicted he would knock out the old fighter.

The match was the talk of the town and brought everyone to ringside. Both boxers were tentative, and it was unlikely that either was sober. Kid Zug kept his hands high to protect his face. Happy's inexperience soon created an opening for the Kid. After he launched a solid right lead and knocked out several of Happy's teeth, the fight was over.

The crowd was surprised but satisfied with the outcome, especially those who had bet on the Kid.

Handsome Andy Stirling, about forty-five, whose duties were vaguely described as "a roustabout", was tall with a boyish face. Some people thought he might be a bodyguard. Stirling wore riding breeches or a business suit. His hard drinking got him into trouble, and he liked to chase after the ladies. When sober he was personable, and he did not let Loren and Sarah see him drunk. Andy was not known to do a day's work, but he called himself Widemann's foreman.

Pescadero was an isolated but lively town. People still cherished the pebbles, and in the village they could have the stones polished in a machine operated by a greyhound dog working a treadmill. Peanuts and popcorn could be bought on the street.

In the summer of 1917 fifty-five-year-old amiable Ed Eaton was killed in a freak car accident. He had left at noon for San Francisco to transact business and rushed home late at night. He fell asleep on the road, and the machine rolled over. A passerby discovered his body, pinned beneath his auto near the Pescadero cemetery. Suspicious people said that Eaton had been sent out on an errand when he was drunk, and that he went over a cliff.

With Ed Eaton out of the picture, Andy Stirling moved up in the hierarchy of Widemann's cohorts. It was said that he would pick the lock on the boss's liquor cabinet. He might have had an opium habit, too, not uncommon during these times when some drugs could be purchased without prescription.

While Widemann's gang was exerting its influence, Loren's household was changing. A middle-aged widow, Mrs. Margaret Harrison, was hired to cook and clean; it is probable that she was brought to town by Widemann. Handyman Joe Quilla milked the cows every morning, and his wife helped out with Wally by taking him for walks. He and his wife lived on North Street near the Coburn house. Although they seemed to keep to themselves, the Quillas saw Sarah daily.

Now in his nineties, Loren was leaving much of his own work, such as inspecting the ranches, to Chris Widemann and his men. Upon the advice of Widemann, Sarah refused permission to anyone to see Loren, knowing he was in the habit of signing his name to any piece of paper he was asked to sign.

Sarah herself was leading a cloistered life, and she was rarely seen away from the house.

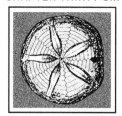

# CHAPTER THIRTY-SIX

# LOREN GOES; SARAH STAYS – 1918

On November 14, 1918, at the close of WWI, Loren Coburn, ninety-two, succumbed to pneumonia at his Pescadero home. Witnesses claimed that Wally, who was now sixty-two, sang an "aimless ditty" about a poor orphaned boy. Loren was buried beside his first wife, Mary Antoinette, at Cypress Lawn Cemetery.

The oldtimer, the unfriendly villager, fell victim to the influenza epidemic that killed 22 million people worldwide. Following the mandate of the Board of Supervisors, Loren tried to protect himself by wearing a gauze mask on San Gregorio Street, but it did not keep out the virus. A villager muttered "the old son of a bitch doesn't want to die yet", when Loren was seen wearing the mask. After all the crusty old man had lived through, he was still hated by some Pescaderans.

The *Coastside Comet* wrote: "Lying at his home in Pescadero seriously ill with pneumonia, Loren Coburn had this to say of Germany's surrender: 'I am glad I was spared long enough to see the end of the war.'"

Loren's obituary described him as the largest individual landowner in San Mateo County. Mention was made that he left behind an "adopted" nephew, Carl Coburn, "the well-known merchant of Pescadero". A fuss was made over Loren's idiosyncrasies, especially his reputation as a tightwad. It was noted that as he lay dying Loren refused to permit Dr. C.V. Thompson to treat him, fearing he would charge too much money. Instead Loren asked for Dr. Morrison, whose office was in San Mateo. When Dr. Morrison came, Loren first interrogated him regarding his fees. He also demanded a written contract to protect Sarah from any unexpected claims for medical services should he die. These stringent measures failed; after Loren's death, Dr. Morrison sued the estate for a thousand dollars; he was awarded eight hundred dollars.

News of Loren's death made the front page of the *Salinas Daily Index*. Under the headline "Loren Coburn's Active Life Comes To A Close", the article described Loren as "...a man of strong likes and dislikes..." and mentioned that the valuable Pescadero ranch had been leased to Widemann.

The *Daily Index* reported that Loren's first will, dated April, 1914, had already been filed. That will was produced in San Francisco "by his widow, immediately after the funeral" at the S.A. White Chapel in San Francisco. With her attorneys Eustace Cullinan, John L. McNab, and Thomas Hickey, Sarah retrieved this "first" will from the bank vaults at the Bank of Italy. In this will, the article continued, "Loren Coburn divided his fortune equally between his widow and his feeble-minded son, except for a one thousand dollar bequest to his 'old and faithful servant Ah Gee'."

In the will Loren explained his motives: "I have in mind those who have been a constant source of trouble to me and who have openly attacked me, and this explains the reason why I have not mentioned relatives other than my wife and son." Witnessing the document were Alfred Gonzales, the president of the Bank of Gonzales, J.H. Skinner, the vice president of the Bank of Italy, and an attorney named Hanley, who drafted the will.

Arzo was one of the mourners at the undertaker's parlor, but it was said that instead of proceeding to the funeral with the others, he rushed to Redwood City and filed a new suit to give himself the Letters of Administration. He asked to be appointed the guardian of Sarah and Wally, citing that neither was competent to handle Loren's complicated estate.

In the first will, dated April, 1914, Sarah and Widemann were named executrix and executor. They were to administer Wally's half of the estate for his benefit and if necessary become his guardians. If Wally died first, his share reverted to Sarah, but if she died first, Wally's half upon his death was to be distributed as follows: ten thousand dollars to the Youth Directory; ten thousand dollars to the Old People's Home; and ten thousand dollars to the Hebrew Home for the Aged and Disabled. The remaining balance was to be shared between Widemann and Ed Eaton and J.A. Bardin, a Monterey County Superior Court Judge. These last three men were said to be friends who showed great acts of kindness and had assisted Loren in time of trouble.

It was learned that since 1914, Widemann had held an option for three hundred and seventy thousand dollars on the Pescadero ranch, which had been appraised at more than four hundred thousand dollars, as well as some seven hundred acres of virgin timber land that had been stripped before the option was given. According to the *San Francisco Chronicle*, Widemann filed the option "...two minutes before five in the afternoon that he [Loren] was dying..." The option, said *Chronicle* sources, was valued at six hundred thousand dollars, and under the terms Widemann could purchase the ranch at any time within ten years for three hundred and seventy thousand dollars. The option was dated March 29, 1914, and witnessed by Widemann's brother. It was awarded three weeks after a San Francisco jury had restored Loren to competency.

As soon as Arzo heard these details, the contest of the wills began. His attorneys, Ross and Ross, pointed out that Widemann's option and lease were evidence that Loren had been too incompetent to manage his own affairs.

Widemann defended himself because other spurious deeds might be filed over which his option would take precedence.

Sarah backed her good friend Widemann. "I have every confidence in Mr. Widemann," she said. "He has done everything possible to develop my husband's property and has expended over two hundred thousand dollars on the Pescadero ranch in recent years."

"As long as the protection of Mrs. Coburn and her son do not demand such action," said Widemann, "I shall never exercise my right of option. I have spent two hundred and fifty-seven thousand dollars developing the property, and that action was all open and above-board. Any suggestion that I now want to cheat these old friends of mine is maliciously absurd."

When told the news that Arzo asked to be appointed her guardian, Sarah snapped: "I think I shall be capable of managing my own business for a while yet. Arzo never brought us anything but trouble and litigation and has been waiting to get a share of the estate for years."

"How dare you say such things about me?" retorted an astonished Arzo. "I am a deacon in the church."

"If you are, God pity the church," spat out Sarah. "The truth is not in you Arzo Coburn. You have been so long unacquainted with it that your tongue is out of practice."

Sarah's legal advisors called Arzo's latest attempt on the property an "outrage on every form of justice". The estate matters would be settled in Superior Court.

As had been the case with Loren himself, new legal documents kept turning up; this time it was a second will. What it contained no one knew at first. There was speculation that Ross and Ross had this will made out after April, 1914. Information that leaked out about this so-called second will said the bulk of the estate had been left to Arzo.

Petitions and counter petitions were filed as well as the applications for guardianship of Sarah and Wally. Sarah's attorneys filed a petition for guardianship of Wally. A petition was also filed by the San Mateo County Public Administrator and Coroner Dr. W.A. Brooke for Special Letters of Administration.

In December, Hall C. Ross filed the mysterious second will, supposedly executed by Loren on October 31, 1914, six months after the first will filed by Sarah. In this second will Arzo was named the executor. Sarah got seventy-five thousand dollars; Wally one hundred thousand dollars in trust...C.L. Littlefield (with whom Loren was in disagreement) was left twenty-five thousand dollars." Carl and Minnie Coburn were the witnesses. Arzo was the "residuary legatee".

A big surprise came when it was announced three months after Loren's death that an agreement had been reached regarding the estate.

"All is serene among the heirs of the aged millionaire," noted the *Times Gazette*. The warring parties met at the County Courthouse to do battle, but instead compromised their financial differences outside of the courtroom. According to the new agreement, Arzo was to inherit one-half of the estate upon the death of Wally. Sarah was to get the other half.

In the first will, upon Wally's death, Sarah was to receive the son's share. If she died before Wally did, his share was to go to the Monterey County Superior Court Judge Bardin and Widemann. In this new agreement, Sarah transferred her rights in the fortune from Wally to Arzo. Widemann did the same. The judge ruled in favor of the first will and ordered it admitted into probate. Before the case was called, Widemann filed an agreement to transfer one-half interest in an option to buy the property for three hundred and seventy-five thousand dollars to Arzo for one hundred thousand dollars. This sum represented one-half the cost of improvements he had made on the property.

H.W. Schaberg, the inheritance tax appraiser for the Loren Coburn estate, filed his inventory and appraisal. He placed the total value at $626,592.00. Cash on hand amounted to $16,770 with two promissory notes appraised for $39,000. The Coburn's Pescadero home was valued at $6,000; the ranch at $375,000; personal effects at $500; the timber ranch at $15,000; timber on it at $152,000; tan bark at $3,000, and property in Merced at $19,312.50.

The executors of Loren's estate paid twenty thousand dollars for the inheritance tax—the largest sum received that year.

Sarah petitioned the Superior Court for a family allowance and funds to provide suitable furniture for her home. The executors also asked the court for an order to sell the personal property of the estate such as old furniture, valued at three hundred dollars, two brown mares worth three hundred dollars, and the two promissory notes valued at thirty-nine thousand dollars. Further, they asked to sell the Merced ranch; the executors said they needed the cash to pay the debts of the estate and to liquidate current expenses.

Now that her husband was dead, Sarah Coburn was seen less frequently, and a veil of mystery surrounded the Coburn house. It was said that Widemann and Andy Stirling kept a constant watch over her, through Mrs. Harrison, and that Sarah had lost her independence. She never traveled to San Francisco or transacted any business unless Widemann or Stirling was with her. It was believed that Widemann feared she might change her will in favor of her relatives.

There was reason for that fear, because Sarah decided to take a long automobile ride "back East" to visit the relatives she had not seen for decades. But who were these relatives? And who had suggested such an extremely difficult trip for a woman in her eighties? Would there be an "accident" on the way? Widemann consented to the trip, but he insisted that Mrs. Harrison accompany her. She was to leave in early June.

Later it was rumored that on June 3, when the County Recorder rang Mrs. Coburn to verify her signature on certain documents—which Sarah denied—Josephine Vosti, filling in as the telephone operator, tipped off Widemann.

Witnesses also later claimed to have seen Chris Widemann and Andy Stirling at a local saloon shaking dice to decide "who will take the old bitch to lunch". And a few days before Sarah was scheduled to leave, Widemann said to Mrs. Harrison, Sarah's constant companion, "You will be going East in a few days. You ought to go to San Francisco and buy any things you need." Mrs. Harrison was reluctant to leave Mrs. Coburn.

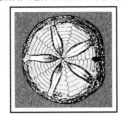

# CHAPTER THIRTY-SEVEN

# THE MURDER

Sarah Coburn did not make the trip "back East" to visit her relatives, although an expensive touring car, a Pierce-Arrow, had been purchased for that ostensible purpose.

Six months after Loren Coburn died, on Wednesday June 4, 1919, the front page of the *San Francisco Call Bulletin* shouted: "Mrs. L. Coburn Found Killed in Home". The *San Mateo News Leader* revealed more of the story in its headlines: "Mrs. Coburn Murdered; Slain While Sleeping in Back Room, Son Found At Her Bedside; Mrs. Harrison, Nurse of The Feeble-Minded Son Away For First Time in Many Months". The *San Francisco Examiner* and the *San Francisco Chronicle* did not ignore the story, nor did the *Salinas Daily Index*: "Wealthy Woman Is Foully Murdered. Mrs. Sarah Coburn Clubbed To Death…"

Joe Quilla, the handyman, discovered the body and called Andy Stirling to the scene, and he called the authorities.

The *Call Bulletin* was reporting a good part of the news of the murder; perhaps this was due to the fact that Matt Sullivan, a one-time journalist with that paper, was the attorney who had defended Arzo Coburn during one of the incompetency trials.

The sixty-three-year-old Wally Coburn did not seem to realize that "Aunt Satira", as he called Sarah, was dead. He was found "muttering incoherently over the lifeless corpse".

Yet witnesses reported him as saying: "I didn't kill anybody. I didn't kill anybody. You kill 'em. I'll bury 'em." District Attorney Franklin Swart, who was busy with the Inez Reed murder case, believed these were the ramblings caused by constant questioning after the slaying.

Under guard, he was taken to Gardiner's Sanitarium for observation.

Nurses at the Sanitarium located in Belmont, between San Mateo and Redwood City, heard him slurring what sounded like the name "Ryan" and the word "killing". The name puzzled authorities. "I know of no one named Ryan who could by the remotest flight of imagination be connected with the case, but Wally keeps repeating the name again and again," said Swart.

Wally also directed threats, according to the *Redwood City Standard*, at R. E. Steele, a colorful wealthy ranchowner who had lost part of his arm in an accident. A big spender and a gambler, whose parents had left him a hefty inheritance, Steele owned the beautiful Cascade Dairy Ranch. Somehow he had made the acquaintance of Charles Humphrey, a San Francisco attorney who was interested in representing Loren Coburn's East Coast relatives.

While in custody Wally received the first haircut he had had in forty-five years. Sheriff Michael Sheehan accompanied him to the barbershop where Wally at first resisted the matron, until they got him to sit quietly in the chair. Then, it was said, he enjoyed the haircut. He was also given his first suit of new clothes in fifty years. He had always worn the castoff clothing of his father.

The District Attorney, the Sheriff, and the County Coroner had all rushed to the scene when they received news of the murder. Swart had been under considerable strain, and jury selection was about to begin in the sensational Inez Reed murder case.

Swart had found the front door unlocked and open, which he said left many things to be explained. Wally was the only other person in the house at the time of the murder, because Mrs. Margaret Harrison had gone to San Francisco on a shopping trip. She explained that she expected to return on the same day, but that afternoon Widemann's chauffeur stopped by to tell her he had to go to Salinas and could not pick her up until Wednesday. We do not know where she was staying in San Francisco. This was the only time Mrs. Harrison had left Sarah and Wally alone.

Mrs. Harrison also mentioned that Sarah had been ill, but "the day I left for San Francisco she was feeling so much better. That is the reason I went."

Swart said robbery was not the motive, because the killer or killers had left behind one thousand six hundred and forty dollars in cash in the big dining room safe. An additional thirty dollars was found in Sarah's handbag in Wally's room.

Dr. Thompson, who performed the autopsy in the house, said that Mrs. Coburn had been beaten to death with a wooden club two feet long. The cause of death was "fracture of the skull…" He said that she would have lived only a few minutes after receiving the blow and that the time of death occurred around 3 a.m.

Dr. Thompson removed the dead woman's stomach for analysis, leaving it in a jar in a Pescadero undertaking establishment.

There was a rush to supply alibis. Mrs. Harrison was in San Francisco. Chris Widemann was in Salinas; Arzo was in Massachusetts, although as soon as he heard the news, he and his wife headed west and then hired detectives to look into the murder.

Carl Coburn said, "I have not been in the Coburn house for ten years. The last time I spoke to Mrs. Sarah Coburn was on December 31 of last year at Redwood City." That was when the contest over the Loren Coburn estate was settled. But there were other villagers who said they saw Carl at the Coburn house often, especially after Loren died. Carl said that he left Pescadero early Wednesday morning and that he first heard the news of Sarah's murder in Redwood City. But it seemed strange that he did not come to Pescadero for twelve hours, not until 9 p.m. of the day Sarah Coburn was murdered. To one newspaper he casually expressed the opinion that Wally may have been the one who committed the murder.

When Swart announced that some bloody clothes had been discovered under a bridge near San Mateo, there was excited speculation that the clothing might lead to the killer—but that lead was soon abandoned.

Coroner William A. Brooke said that he had found a will, dated February 27, 1919, in a purse in Wally's room. It was signed by Sarah.

According to the *San Mateo News Leader* the will read as follows:

"SARAH SATIRA COBURN, BEING OF LAWFUL AGE AND OF SOUND AND DISPOSING MIND AND NOT ACTING UNDER DURESS, MENACE, FRAUD OR UNDER UNDUE INFLUENCE OF ANY PERSON OR PERSONS DO HEREBY MAKE, PUBLISH AND DECLARE THIS MY LAST WILL AND TESTAMENT, TO WIT:

1. I HEREBY REVOKE ALL FORMER WILLS MADE BY ME.

2. I GIVE, DEVISE AND BEQUEATH UNTO MY FRIENDS, C.H. WIDEMANN AND J.A. BARDIN, THE EQUAL AND UNDIVIDED ONE-HALF OF ALL PROPERTY OF WHICH I DIE THE OWNER OF, WHETHER SAME IS REAL, PERSONAL OR MIXED, OR IN WHICH I HAVE ANY INTEREST, OF ANY KIND OR CHARACTER, WHEREVER SITUATED, IN CONSIDERATION OF THEIR FRIENDSHIP FOR ME, AND IN CONSIDERATION THAT THEY GAVE UP THEIR LEGACIES UNDER THE WILL OF LOREN COBURN AT MY REQUEST.

3. I GIVE TO WALLACE LOREN COBURN THE INCOME AND PROFITS OF THE SUM OF $50,000 AS LONG AS HE SHALL LIVE, AND I DIRECT THAT PAID SUM OF $50,000 BE SET ASIDE BY MY EXECUTORS HEREINAFTER NAMED IN TRUST TO MY SAID EXECUTORS, AND THAT AS SAID TRUSTEES THEY SHALL APPLY THE SAID INCOME FOR THE BEST INTEREST AND BENEFIT OF SAID WALLACE LOREN COBURN DURING HIS LIFE, AND AT THE DEATH OF SAID WALLACE LOREN COBURN SAID TRUST SHALL THEN TERMINATE AND SAID TRUSTEES SHALL TURN THE REMAINDER OF THE SUM OF $50,000 OVER TO MY FRIEND C.H. WIDEMANN FOR HIS OWN USE AND BENEFIT.

4. I GIVE TO MY HOUSEKEEPER MRS. HARRISON, THE SUM OF $2,500.

5. I GIVE TO MRS. EATON, THE WIDOW OF MY DECEASED FRIEND E.A. EATON, THE SUM OF $5,000.

6. I GIVE TO MY FRIEND JOHN L. MCNAB, THE SUM OF $1,000.

7. I GIVE TO MY FRIEND C.H. WIDEMANN, IN RECOGNITION OF MANY SERVICES RENDERED ME BY HIM, ALL OF THE REST, RESIDUE AND REMAINDER OF MY ESTATE OF EVERY KIND, AND IN CASE OF HIS DEATH BEFORE ME, TO HIS HEIRS.

8. I NOMINATE AND APPOINT C.H. WIDEMANN AND J.A. BARDIN EXECUTORS OF THIS, MY LAST WILL AND TESTAMENT, TO SERVE WITHOUT BONDS.

IN WITNESS WHEREOF I HAVE HEREUNTO SET MY HAND AND SEAL THIS 27TH DAY OF FEBRUARY, 1919, IN THE PRESENCE OF JOSEPHINE A. VOSTI AND ANDREW J. STIRLING, WHOM I HAVE REQUESTED TO BECOME ATTESTING WITNESSES HERETO.

(SIGNED) SARAH SATIRA COBURN

Later, Dr. Brooke filed a petition for Special Letters of Administration, stating that "an instrument purporting to be the will" of Mrs. Coburn disposes of the entire estate to "strangers in blood", with the exception of a temporary provision for Wally.

A jury of Pescaderans was summoned by Dr. Brooke for the coroner's report. As the prime suspect, Wally was at the center of the inquiry. Mrs. Margaret Harrison was one of those who testified.

She was asked whether Wally could carry on a conversation.

"Sometimes he would be able to carry on a little conversation, but he would gradually drift away from it."

"Could you send him for anything?"

"No," said Mrs. Harrison. "If you would ask him to shut the door, he would take no notice of it. He never liked to see the pantry door open and would often shut it, but if you asked him to do it, he would not do it."

"Would he ever express himself as having a certain thing on his mind and do it?"

"If he wanted to go out and walk on the porch, he would get his hat and go."

"Did he ever show a tendency to be violent?"

"When you crossed him, he probably would."

"Did he ever pick up anything and threaten to use it on you?"

"Yes, he did once. I wanted him to go to bed, and he didn't want to. He was on the floor in his bare feet. I told him he must get to bed, or he would catch cold and get sick. He took a poker and said he was going to strike me with it. I took it away from him, and he dropped his hands and gave up."

"Had Mrs. Coburn and Wally been friendly lately?"

"Yes. I think Wally thought a great deal of Mrs. Coburn. Sarah had always been very kind to him."

"Have you ever noticed him to pick up wood out of the wood box?"

"He has, yes. He threatened to strike Mrs. Coburn once; Joe, our man, brings in the wood everyday."

"From what you have observed from the boy, could you conceive of him going to get the stick and striking Mrs. Coburn?"

"I don't think he would do it unless he was crossed."

"Could he remember anything from one day to the next?"

"No," said Mrs. Harrison, "he would forget. His mind runs in the past."

"Was he in the habit of getting up at night?"

"Yes, about six o'clock."

"Did he call for Mrs. Coburn?"

"Yes, if she didn't hear him, he would get up."

"Suppose she had been alone and not responded to his requests, would that have irritated him?"

"He would mumble to himself, then get up."

"Do you know of any reason why anybody should want to do harm to Mrs. Coburn?"

"I don't know. I don't know many people around here."

"Did she go out a great deal?"

"She used to go out in the backyard in the evenings a good deal. I used to tell her not to stay out there so late…"

"Was she accustomed to leave the door open at night?"

"No. She always locked the door. She would lock both screens and the inner door."

"Did Wally ever unlock the inner door?"

"She told me he used to, but I have never seen him do it." She said she did not know of anyone else who would and noted again that Mrs. Coburn never went to bed without locking the door. "She used to put the large rocking chair against the door."

"Do you think Wally could of got up in the night and opened the door?"

"I don't think so. I think Mrs. Coburn could of heard him, and besides he cannot get along very well in the dark." She said that Mrs. Coburn always kept a light burning at night. "She used to set the lamp near the door. She would put it out in the morning. Lately Mrs. Coburn had been complaining with her arm, so she used to get up early, between half past seven and eight o'clock…"

"She always kept her door open?"

"Yes." Mrs. Harrison said she herself slept in a room off the kitchen.

"Wally would usually get up about half past six to relieve himself?"

"Yes. He would use the chamber at the foot of his bed."

"He would usually call for somebody to help him?"

"Yes. If you were around, he would think you ought to help him, but if he was alone, he would wait upon himself."

"Has anyone called her within the last two or three weeks in reference to business matters?"

Mrs. Harrison said no and that Mrs. Coburn didn't have any visitors or callers.

"Had Mrs. Coburn ever discussed with you any past experiences with the son in cases where he injured anybody?"

"I think she was very sensitive about that. Someone told me one time about him striking somebody. She would never tell me, because she was afraid I would go away."

"Did you ever know of his using violence toward Mr. Coburn?"

"I heard that Mr. Coburn had a black eye. I don't know if that is true or not. You hear so many things around this town. The town is all right, I guess, but it's the people in it."

Joe Quilla, the Portuguese handyman and milkman, was asked if "the boy" liked him. "Yes, I used to be afraid of him though," he added with a heavy accent.

"Did he ever bother you?"

"No, but they said he would do anything."

When Andy Stirling took the stand, he revealed that Mrs. Coburn intended to go back east on June 8 and that he was going to travel with her.

"Did you ever see him [Wally] threaten violence?"

"Yesterday, or the day before, he kind of threatened to do violence. He was driving some nails into a plank, some burnt nails, and I gave him some more. Then Mrs. Coburn came out and said something to him, and he began to cry. He called her an S.B."

"Did he have the hammer in his hands?"

"Yes. Mrs. Coburn said: 'Now, Wally, don't do that!' Then he began to holler to beat the band. He ran down the street and they brought him back."

"Would you say he carried any feeling against Mrs. Coburn?"

"He was very friendly toward Mrs. Harrison, but he seemed irritable toward Mrs. Coburn. He has made several remarks against Mrs. Coburn. About six weeks ago, Mrs. Coburn told him to do something, and he became very irritable and swore at her."

"Do you remember the position of the stick [the murder weapon] when you found it?"

"One end of the stick was shaped like a handle. I think this end was on the outside, but I am not sure..."

"When the boy got angry, he never kept his anger for any length of time, did he?"

"No, he soon forgot it."

"The day he ran away and was brought back, was he very cross?"

"No, he was all right then. When anything like that would happen he would be all right afterwards."

"Do you know of Wally using violence at any time?"

"He struck Mr. Coburn once, and made a swing at Mrs. Coburn with the poker, then dropped his hand."

"Did Mrs. Coburn go away a short time ago to collect some money a party owed her for rent..."

"Yes, she went to Merced and got a check from him for twelve hundred dollars."

"How do you know it was twelve hundred dollars?"

"She told me. Coming home, she showed me a roll of bills. She said, 'We can have lots of fun with all that money.'"

"Where was it she showed you the roll of bills?"

"Just outside the city."

"Has she had occasion to go to any bank since that time?"

"No, I don't think she has left the house since then. She had a pretty good sized roll."

"That was two weeks ago?"

"Yes. She must have had that hid. She hasn't been in any banks. She has been out to take one or two rides in her limousine since then. I am positive she has been no where else."

Widemann concurred that Mrs. Coburn had cashed a check for twelve hundred dollars.

"She took it from the bank," he said, "and then came home a day or two later."

"You knew Wally quite well?"

"Yes."

"Did you ever know of Wally using violence on anybody?"

"No."

"Did you ever know of his having any special grievance toward Mrs. Coburn?"

"He liked Mrs. Harrison a little better than he did Mrs. Coburn…"

"Do you think Wally did that [murdered Sarah]?"

"I don't know. I would like to say he did."

"Do you know whether Mrs. Coburn left a will?"

"I think she did." He said he thought it was in the safe.

"Do you know of anyone who would profit by her death?"

"I do not."

"Was she accustomed to cashing large checks?"

"She used to get money for rent in the East, and I used to cash them right along for her."

"She cashed all her checks?"

"Yes. She may have deposited some in the bank."

After all the testimony was received, the verdict was rendered that "said deceased came to her death from a blow on the head by a piece of wood exhibited to the jury, by some person unknown to them, thereby causing a fracture of the skull." Dr. Brooke said the jury did not find enough evidence to convict Wally for the murder. Among the jurors were J.C. Williamson, A.W. Woodham, J.J. Machado, J.A. McCormick, M.J. Perry, Frank Montevaldo, G.S. Winkler, and C.L. Littlefield.

Many Pescaderans who knew "the boy" regarded him as harmless;

they did not believe he was a murderer.

Suddenly the village was overrun with detectives. The Western Detective Agency was working on the case for Arzo, who was on his way to the village, and another set of detectives were hard at work, but District Attorney Swart refused to say who was paying them. Widemann hired two sets of detectives to check the operations of the others, and a fifth group of detectives had been hired by the *San Francisco Examiner*.

The San Francisco authorities, Chief of Police White, Detectives Frank McConnell and Charles Gallivan as well as special Policewoman Katherine "Kate" O'Connor, were dispatched to the scene. Their interest in the case stemmed from evidence that part of the crime may have been hatched in San Francisco, in their jurisdiction. With them in the automobile rushing to the scene was attorney Eustace Cullinan, one of Sarah's attorneys, now working for Widemann.

The professional detectives and private investigators filled the one hotel and every lodging house in Pescadero.

"We have circumstantial evidence against the slayer," Swart said soon after the murder, "but it would be unwise to make an arrest without sufficient evidence to convict. 'The boy', as they call him, was never resentful. He had no power to remember an injury, and he had no conception of money or what it means. That he could murder his stepmother seems preposterous."

Mrs. Harrison, in the presence of San Francisco Policewoman Kate O'Connor, concurred that Wally could not have committed the murder.

But when asked what the motive was for killing Sarah, no one in Pescadero gave "a proper answer".

Sarah's body was buried at Cypress Lawn Cemetery, beside that of her husband. Rev. S.J. Lee, rector of St. James Protestant Episcopal Church in San Francisco, conducted the service. The Knickerbocker Quartet sang. Some thirty-five friends accompanied the body to the cemetery; Widemann and Eustace Cullinan were among them.

Carl Coburn was not silent during this time; he and his father were eyeing property they wished to buy east of Pescadero; it was the former house of the Haywards, a prominent lumbering family. Chris Widemann's brother, Honore, had appeared in the village. He met one of Carl's daughters, and a romance evolved into marriage and children. Now a grandfather, Carl Coburn developed a new relationship with Chris Widemann.

# THE WILL

On the Sunday after the murder, automobiles invaded the village of Pescadero, and people stopped to stare at the cottage where the crime took place.

One theory behind Sarah's murder was that it emanated from the contested will. The *Examiner*, which had detectives working on the case, reported that "the aged widow lived to keep coin from kin and probably had not an idea of what she intended to do with it, except that she wanted to prevent the relatives of Loren Coburn from getting it." She wanted to live long enough—and to keep Wally alive—to prevent Arzo from grabbing a share of the estate.

By the terms of the settlement of the contested will, Sarah got her half, and Arzo agreed to abandon the contest if the other half of the estate held in trust during Wally's life would go to him at Wally's death.

Since Wally could not make a will, attorney John L. McNab said that Arzo was in line for a large portion of the estate. But Arzo's attorney, Lee Ross, countered that his client was not the sole beneficiary, because Arzo's interest had already been settled out of court, and he would receive nothing from Sarah's will.

In the days following the murder, blame began to shift away from Wally. The general view was that it was done by someone outside of the family. "The whole plan of the murder is being cleared before us," said Swart, the District Attorney. "The man who killed Mrs. Coburn planned the crime with the idea that suspicion would be fixed on Wally..."

Six detectives employed by the East Coast heirs of the Coburn estate said that Wally could not have committed the murder. The authorities themselves did not believe that Wally could have committed the murder without staining himself with blood.

"I am firm in my belief that Wallace Coburn did not strike and kill his stepmother," said Swart. "While there is little hope of obtaining a sane statement from him, the private investigation is proceeding satisfactorily.

"I am not in a position to reveal the lines in which the investigation is being conducted. But I will say that the finger of suspicion is pointing toward a certain person and that there is every likelihood of an arrest being made within the next two days."

During the investigation, Andy Stirling and other members of Widemann's clan, including "Kid Zug", were questioned. It was learned that Widemann and Stirling had planned to accompany Sarah Coburn back East to inspect property that she was interested in buying.

On another occasion, Swart said: "You may say that I have secured evidence pointing to one person, implicating at least one more, as the murderers of Mrs. Coburn and that an arrest will be made soon."

But there was no arrest. It must be remembered that in the early days of the investigation, when the murder had the best chance of being solved, Swart was preparing to go to trial in the Inez Reed case. In early July Swart won that case; Dr. Northcott was found guilty and sentenced to San Quentin.

A week after Sarah Coburn's murder there was a report that the wooden club used as the murder weapon had disappeared—and then reappeared when Sheriff Michael Sheehan said that he had had the weapon all along. Also missing and never found was the dead woman's stomach, removed during the autopsy by Dr. Thompson.

Ten days after the body was discovered, the District Attorney said that "an article found in the Coburn home following the murder has been traced to the owner, and we have secured his fingerprints...We are still at a loss to know whether revenge or robbery was the motive that prompted the crime. An arrest will be made soon, but to arrest the man we are now watching would make it possible for the man who planned the crime with him to escape. Until the arrest I will have nothing further to say. The stage of talking is past."

But no arrests were made.

A month after the murder, Sarah's will was admitted to probate by Judge George Buck. Taking the stand were Andy Stirling and Josephine Vosti, whose names appeared as witnesses on the document. Within days the will was declared a forgery by handwriting experts Chauncey McGovern and Carl Eisenschimmel. Both men were well respected. With an office at 830 Market Street, Eisenschimmel worked for the San Francisco Police Department and wrote articles for the *Police Journal* on subjects such as "Handwriting & Crime".

The dashing San Francisco attorney and land developer, Charles Franklin Humphrey, who had lived with his family in Europe for eight years, jumped into the case. Armed with reports from the handwriting experts, Humphrey went to Massachusetts to consult with twenty heirs, all of them Loren's relatives, regarding a new contest of the will.

Said Eustace Cullinan, Widemann's attorney: "...Attorney Humphrey is merely making a private speculation in the hope that he might manage to break the will. He has been trying to get some of the heirs to go fifty-fifty with him if he could knock out the will. I have in my possession a letter written by Humphrey to Carl Coburn...in which Humphrey agreed to give Carl one-seventh of his fee if Carl would induce his foster father, J.C. Coburn, to employ him to fight the case. Carl Coburn turned the offer down, and now Humphrey has gone East to try to persuade some of the other relatives to start something. I am absolutely sure we can prove the will is authentic. We can prove Mrs. Coburn made the will and also that she made subsequent statements proving that she made it."

After studying copies of Sarah's handwriting and a photo of the signatures attached to the will given to him by Humphrey, Chauncey McGovern proclaimed the signature was forged. He asked that his conclusions be confirmed by Carl Eisenschimmel. Humphrey advised District Attorney Swart to carry on the investigation.

The will in question had been typed on a typewriter of "ancient vintage", and only the signature was written. It was not known if Mrs. Coburn owned or knew how to use a typewriter. The letter and the alignment indicated that it was not written by a stenographer in a lawyer's office, according to the handwriting experts.

"I have examined in the records at Redwood City more than a dozen admitted signatures of Mrs. Coburn," Eisenschimmel told the *San Francisco Examiner*. "Some of them were on the outside folders of documents. Five of them were signed by her in her full name of Sarah Satira Coburn, and from these signatures compared with the purported signatures in the will, I have no hesitancy in declaring that the latter signature was a crude fabrication not embodying any of the characteristics or mannerisms of Mrs. Coburn's known writing..."

An example of the facsimile of the signature on the will and the admitted signatures, the handwriting experts said, showed several variations upon which they based their opinion. In admitted signatures the initial "S" and the following "a" were not connected as they were in the alleged forgery. In the original the "a" was made with one stroke, instead of two, as in the will. The final "h" in Sarah faded out in a flourish on the real signature. In the will it seemed to be a drawn line.

Widemann's lawyer, Cullinan, said that his clients had been Sarah's friends for many years and had helped to build up Loren's properties. When Loren died—and a contested will was imminent—Widemann, and Bardin, to save Sarah from further litigation, waived their rights under Loren's will. To show her appreciation, Sarah provided for Widemann and Bardin in this will and allegedly told others that she had done so.

The claims of forgery brought the matter into court with new attempts to break the will.

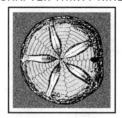

# CHAPTER THIRTY-NINE

# THE WILL CONTESTED

Six months after the death of Sarah Coburn, a contest of the Loren Coburn will was filed by his son Wally and his only surviving brother J.C. Superior Court Judge George Buck set the contest for hearing. The contestants charged that Loren was incompetent when he made the will, dividing his estate between Widemann and Monterey County Judge Bardin. Loren's nephew, Arzo, was not involved in this contest, because Widemann had already given him property valued at two hundred thousand dollars to avert an earlier contest of the will.

As proof that Widemann used "undue influence" in having himself named executor, the contestants pointed to that earlier settlement with Arzo. They said that "when Arzo came to the coast after the murder of Sarah Satira Coburn, Widemann sent word to him that he wanted to see him. When Arzo called on Widemann, Widemann conveyed to him two pieces of property in Fitchburg, Massachusetts; assigned him the fifty thousand dollars legacy left for Wally; and Judge Bardin agreed to give him a promissory note for ten thousand dollars—all of this in order to avert a contest, even though Arzo was not a direct heir nor entitled to inherit under the Sarah Satira will."

Now Wally had three guardians: J.C., Widemann, and Dr. Brooke. Dr. Brooke, "in bringing this contest," said Eustace Cullinan, "is really representing the Eastern relatives of Loren Coburn, who are not the relatives of Mrs. Coburn at all." He added that Mrs. Coburn "knew that if she left her estate to the imbecile nephew, Wallace Coburn, he would be unable to make a will, and her estate would go ultimately to these Eastern relatives of Loren Coburn, who had been at enmity with Mrs. Coburn for many years." He said Mrs. Coburn's signature on the will was authentic. "The contestants," noted Cullinan, "showed how little faith they have in the forgery charge by adding to their contest charges of undue influence and incompetence..."

J.C. Coburn filed an action against Widemann, to set aside the option for the purchase of the Coburn ranch. The contest of the will was dismissed after an agreement was reached with the Eastern heirs, who were to take a portion of the balance of the estate left upon Wally's death. Widemann exercised his option to buy the ranch and paid three hundred and seventy-five thousand dollars into the estate; appraised value of the property was about six hundred thousand dollars. The Eastern heirs were paid a cash sum, the amount undisclosed, and they would receive a portion of whatever remained at Wally's death.

Was it possible that Wally would outlive them all?

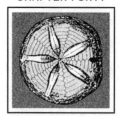

# CHAPTER FORTY

# WHO DID IT?

Renewed efforts to catch the murderer of Sarah Coburn revived in the fall. In a series of all-night sessions, District Attorney Swart interrogated Margaret Harrison, Chris Widemann, Josie Vosti, Frank Zug, Fanny Eaton, John Clements, and J.F. Wooding, (the chauffeur at the time of the murder.) The San Francisco Police came back on the case, summoning the identical witnesses in an effort to solve the crime first. As if orchestrated, the witnesses painted Wally as a violent person capable of anything.

Fanny Eaton, whose husband had been killed in an automobile accident and who now lived in Oakland, told San Francisco Lt. Charles Goff that at times Wally was violent and that in her presence he had made frequent threats against Sarah. Margaret Harrison changed her testimony again and said that Wally could have murdered his stepmother.

Since the murder, she explained, "I have heard Wally say several times, 'I killed Auntie. I knocked her with a stick.' " She said that she heard Wally say it to Dr. Thompson and threaten to knock the doctor's head off.

"There are those witnesses who will testify that Wallace Coburn has told them of the murder," said Eustace Cullinan, Widemann's attorney. He said that "John E. Quinn, a teacher in the West Lake Academy, who drove Wally from the sanatarium, will testify having heard him say, 'I killed Aunty Sally with a wooden club.' " Dr. Thompson, who was keeping a close watch over Wally, who was living at home, reported hearing a similar remark.

Swart had put "the boy" through a test where he was subjected to a three-hour ordeal, where every means to arouse a spirit of violence in him was used. He failed to respond and remained impassive. He could not even identify photographs of Loren and Sarah. Wally was definitely ruled out as the slayer.

Mrs. Florence Petits, whose husband was in charge of Widemann's goat ranch, reported that on the night of the murder she saw "a mysterious man" walking past the Coburn house, a man who acted strangely and did not wear an overcoat, which seemed odd during the cold night. Mrs. Petit's testimony led to a hearing, but nothing further came of it.

In late September "Kid Zug" was accused of beating Frank Goularte, the 190-pound son of the Pescadero blacksmith. Then about age forty, Goularte suffered black eyes, a fractured nose, and bruises on his face and head.

"I was on my way to a dance at Woodruff Inn," said Goularte. "Before going there I stopped at San Gregorio to get a shave, and when I left the shop...the Kid attacked me".

Goularte appeared before the Justice-of-the-Peace in Redwood City and charged Zug with battery. A date for trial was set, and the Kid went before a jury. The evidence at the trial showed that the attack had indeed occurred, but the jury decided that Zug's actions were justifiable. The testimony revealed that Goularte had made offensive remarks directed at Zug and made a move as if he were to draw for a gun. Zug was acquitted.

Insiders knew the truth. Goularte, whom the Pescaderans considered a "troublemaker", was also a significant witness in the murder investigation: he had told the authorities that he saw Andy Stirling go into Sarah's house late on the night of the murder.

Another plot against Goularte involved some false affidavits by Zug and Jockey Baker, a chauffeur and another member of Widemann's household. The affidavits claimed that Goularte approached them at a dance in La Honda and offered each a five-hundred-dollar bribe if they would testify to seeing Stirling run away from the Coburn house the night of the murder.

Goularte was also charged with burglary, but the case was dismissed for lack of evidence. He was accused of stealing sixteen dollars from Perry Ferris, a Pescadero trapper. Ferris admitted being drunk at the time and not certain exactly how much money had been stolen. He said he had been told that Goularte was the one who entered his room at the Swanton House and took the money from his trouser pocket. He further testified that the affidavit which he signed at the suggestion of Andy Stirling was drawn up at Widemann's house by Dr. Thompson.

The chief complaining witness, L. Cardoza, said that he, too, was with Goularte on the night of the burglary; but he admitted he had merely signed an affidavit drawn up for him in the Widemann house.

The attempts to make Wally think he had committed the murder and to discredit the witness Frank Goularte had failed; now the case took a strange turn. The authorities speculated boldly on whom they believed was the slayer and on who might have conceived the crime.

"I know that certain parties," said Andy Stirling, "are trying to fasten this murder on me, but it is all a frame-up." Stirling joked freely about the suspicions pointed in his direction. At one juncture, after an all-night interrogation session with Swart in Redwood City, he walked into the county jail and laughingly asked William Hogan, the jailer: "Bill, have you got a good room here? I'm going to be with you soon, for murder."

Andy Stirling became a suspect, but he was not arrested for the crime. San Francisco Police Lt. Goff and Policewoman Kate O'Connor visited Sarah's home in search of more clues, but they found nothing. Lurid stories began to surface. It was said that Stirling was drunk one night after the murder, when someone remarked that it was a wonder Mrs. Coburn didn't struggle more. Allegedly he replied: "Hell, her leg twitched and that was all."

People whispered that Dr. Thompson was in on the crime and that he put drugs in Sarah's food; that would explain the disappearance of her stomach after the autopsy.

Closeted with Swart and Lt. Goff, Widemann promised his full cooperation. Goff said that Stirling would have to account for his movements over the past three years. It was known that he had lived in Salinas and then suddenly moved to Spokane, Washington, where he was suspected of using "dope". Gus Lapierre, the chef and owner of the Hotel Bardin in Salinas, was questioned regarding his friendship with Stirling.

Joe Quilla, the ranchhand, was heard by detectives to say: "When I saw Wallace and noticed there was no blood on his hands, Stirling said to me, 'You keep your damn mouth shut.' "

Worried about what an inebriated Stirling would announce to the patrons at the Elkhorn Saloon, Widemann locked him in his house in Pescadero but allowed him to uncork his stock of liquor. Stirling was reportedly demanding large sums of money from Widemann, and a break was coming between them.

On cue, Swart attempted to break down Stirling during several interview sessions, in spite of Widemann's increased vigilance. There were rumors that Stirling would be eliminated, as Ed Eaton had been: that is, sent out in an automobile while drunk. Also, since the murder, a Mrs. Betts, who lived in Pescadero, was under surveillance. She was believed to know the whole story through an affair with one of Widemann's chauffeurs, John Clements. She said that she heard Andy Stirling say before the murder, "I will get rid of the old bitch if I have to dump her over a cliff."

The person very likely to have known the whole story was Josie Vosti, Widemann's secretary and a witness to the purported will. San Francisco Policewoman Kate O'Connor was assigned to interrogate Josie, but nothing came of it.

After being released from the sanitarium, Wally was living at the house again. In charge of his medical care was Dr. Thompson. It was believed that at any trial Dr. Thompson would testify that Wally had vicious tendencies and could have murdered Sarah. He and a male nurse teased and antagonized Wally every day. They would put a club in his hand and encourage him to believe that he "murdered Aunt Satira". But there was no trial.

Andy Stirling was disliked and feared after Sarah's murder. He reportedly told people "I'm getting some money" after the murder; it was thought to be around twenty-five thousand dollars. It terrified the Pescaderans to think that he had wielded the bloody wooden club. There were also rumors that Judge Buck and District Attorney Swart received sudden windfalls in the form of "quails stuffed with cash".

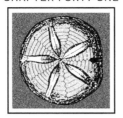

# CHAPTER FORTY-ONE

# ZUG'S STORY

Solving the Coburn murder seemed to have been all but forgotten when two years later there was a sudden burst of interest; once again the San Francisco and the San Mateo County Police believed an arrest was imminent. Successful prosecution in the case was based on the validity of statements made by Frank "Kid" Zug to detectives in San Francisco. He had been a leading figure in the previous investigation, best known for having provided comic relief. Disgusted, Zug announced he had been "used long enough as a tool for Widemann's dirty work". Now he wanted to tell his side of the story.

Zug's explosive affidavit alleged that Widemann induced him to beat Frank Goularte, also a main witness in the murder and the man who said that he had seen Andy Stirling enter the Coburn house late the night of the murder.

Now working for a Sausalito real estate company, Zug's whereabouts were known only to the police.

"This thing is going to break," promised District Attorney Swart, who was not ready to make an arrest, "but it is something that cannot be done hurriedly. The case is too grave, and there is too much at stake to rush into it. Arrests based on Zug's affidavit are very probably in the near future, but there are a number of rights and phases of this case that in my opinion must be investigated with the utmost care before any official move can be made."

From November 1918 to March 1920 Zug worked as a painter for Widemann; he worked very little, but Widemann always paid him. He fell ill with pneumonia during the last stages of the influenza epidemic in

May of 1919 and was admitted to the county hospital in San Mateo; he was released on June 1, a few days before Sarah's murder. Dr. Thompson motored him back to Pescadero, where he spent the evenings of June 1, 2, and 3 at Widemann's house. Widemann was out of town on those three nights.

The first night Dr. Thompson, Tony Vierra, a highway patrolman, and Andy Stirling were there. Stirling drank heavily and encouraged Zug to join him. Stirling talked incessantly about Sarah Coburn and how much property she was going to leave him; he even said that she was "stuck" on him and that he could marry her if he wanted to. These were startling revelations. Stirling claimed that Wally tried to kill her; that he had become vicious lately and would hammer nails all over the house. He produced arm straps which had been used to restrain "the boy".

Towards midnight, Dr. Thompson suggested that Tony and Frank go home together. It was cold, and Stirling loaned Zug his overcoat; the summer months in Pescadero have cool sea fogs that come in during the mornings and evenings.

On the evening of June third, when Sarah was murdered, Dr. Thompson, Stirling, and Zug drank heavily again. Zug was told to go home, which he did. This was before supper, and Zug got his supper at the Swanton House where he roomed. About 7 p.m. Zug, who was weak from his illness, went to his room to sleep. On the way he passed Andy Stirling who said he was going to the Coburn house, "to put the old lady to bed." Zug said, "Rub yourself in good," knowing that Andy always rubbed Sarah's arm, which was sore and painful.

Zug related that he fell asleep, but near midnight he was awakened by the loud braying of bloodhounds and other dogs that were running from the Swanton House to the Coburn house and back past the hotel to Widemann's house and back again. This happened at least a dozen times, he recalled.

He woke up about 7:30 a.m. After breakfast in the kitchen, he walked to Carl Coburn's store, the Emporium, and sat on the porch with Ed Gayety. Constable Fry dropped by, and Zug mentioned the barking dogs. Fry said that he knew nothing about it. About 8 or 8:30 a.m. Zug saw Andy going to the Coburn house and called to him, but Andy did not stop, nor did he stop when Zug called to him again, as he returned with Dr. Thompson.

Gayety bet a dollar that the old lady was dead. Then Andy and Dr. Thompson walked out of the Coburn house and went to the Doctor's house. From there Andy went to the McCormick store and then to Widemann's office, passing Zug and Gayety. Andy whispered to Zug that the old lady was dead, that Wally had killed her, but to say nothing about it. Zug followed Andy back to the McCormick store; the telephone rang. Andy took it down and said that the newspapers wanted to know about Sarah's death. He asked Zug what he should say. "Tell them she was murdered," he coached. Nervously, Andy told the reporter that Sarah had been killed and that it looked like the "half wit" stepson did it.

Later that day Zug and Stirling congregated with others at Widemann's house. Stirling started drinking heavily again. When everyone left, Widemann scolded him: "Andy, for God's sake, quit your drinking and cut out that talk."

After the murder, Zug said that Stirling asked him to find out what people were saying about him. Zug reported back that, while nobody was accusing him of the crime, they thought he was the one who killed the old lady.

Zug said that Widemann suggested that he should start a fist-fight with Frank Goularte, the blacksmith, giving reasons such as "He was playing detective" and, "He was no good anyway". Widemann and Dr. Thompson repeatedly asked Zug to "get something" on Goularte; they wanted to frame him and put him in the penitentiary. They wanted to get something on his father, Manuel, who also had seen Stirling enter the Coburn house on the night of the murder. Zug was ordered to knock the old man out with a club; he refused to obey.

Stirling's idea was for Zug to say that he had seen Goularte burglarize trapper Perry Ferris's room at the Swanton House; Zug refused. Stirling got the job done without Zug.

After that first evening when Stirling loaned Zug his overcoat to wear, Zug had kept it. At noon on the fourth day, Zug could not find the overcoat. When he learned it was missing, Stirling became furious and demanded to know where it was. Zug said it was gone. The next morning Zug found another one of Stirling's overcoats in his room, and he wore that one for three or four days. But it also disappeared, and he did not see it again until the night of the investigation at Redwood City; Stirling then gave him back the second overcoat and his hat to wear.

Zug's affidavit presented the investigators with entirely new information and a reason to proceed with the case.

Meanwhile during that summer of 1920, Loren Coburn's huge land holdings at Pescadero were subdivided into small farms by the Peninsula Farms Company, which had secured control of the badly managed property from Widemann.

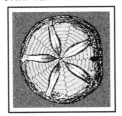

# CHAPTER FORTY-TWO

# THE FIRST FIRE

On a late windless evening in November of 1921, a fire started in the Widemann Garage, on part of the Coburn place on San Gregorio Street. It spread to the Coastside Transportation Company on one side and the Coburn house on the other side. Inside the house was Wally, who was taken from his bed by his "keeper" and Widemann's sometime chauffeur, J.W. Gooding, and the housekeeper, Margaret Harrison. Most of the furnishings were saved.

For a time the fire, started from undetermined causes, threatened to destroy the entire village. The flames were raging by the time the fire was discovered. There was no organized fire department; there was no fire-fighting equipment. It took the combined efforts of every resident who responded to the sound of the alarm, many of them carrying buckets and hoses. A bucket brigade was formed, and streams of water from the largest hose, which was immersed in the creek, were sprayed onto adjoining buildings. There were attempts to move automobiles and goods stored in the garages, but the presence of gasoline and oil made it dangerous. A truck, two automobiles, and a hearse were destroyed. By midnight the fire was under control.

The Widemann Garage, the Coastside Transportation Company garage, and Loren Coburn's old residence, which was Wally's home, were destroyed in the conflagration. Paint was scorched on nearby buildings, and the plate glass windows in the Williamson store were cracked by the heat.

As usual, Widemann was out of town during the fire, and everyone noticed that he, as if by pre-arrangement, could never be found at the scene of any disaster.

Some good came out of the fire: new fire-fighting equipment was acquired in Pescadero: a pump and three thousand feet of three-inch pipe, with three hundred feet of fire hose, were installed. The pump would raise water from the Pescadero Creek to supply a large tank in the back of J.C. Williamson's general store. The pipeline stretched four hundred feet along San Gregorio Street and six hundred feet on Ocean Avenue up to "the hospital" owned by Dr. Thompson.

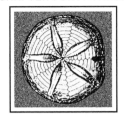

# CHAPTER FORTY-THREE

# THE CASE IN JUDGE O'BRIEN'S COURT

The Coburn murder case was revived by William F. Herrin, the once-powerful chief counsel for the Southern Pacific Railroad. Earlier, the *Los Angeles Times* described him: "While such men...cumber the earth and are able to pursue their infamous conspiracies against the public good, it is the imperative duty of all honest men of all parties to be vigilant in checkmating their schemes and counter-acting...their influence for evil."

But Herrin's time as a political dictator had passed by in 1910. He still lived near Nob Hill in San Francisco, where the Big Four, who founded the Southern Pacific Railroad, built beautiful homes, and he favored William Keith landscape paintings purchased from the exclusive Gump's store on Post Street.

Herrin was hired as counsel by the East Coast heirs, and he loudly accused Widemann and Stirling as the murderers of Sarah Coburn—something others only whispered about. He swore out a murder complaint and applied for warrants for both men.

There were rumors that Widemann was on the run, on the East Coast heading for Europe; Stirling was known to be in San Francisco.

To San Francisco Police Judge Daniel S. O'Brien, Herrin explained that he applied for warrants in San Francisco because Section 781 of the *Penal Code* provided that when part of a plot leading to the crime was committed in another county, either county had jurisdiction. He believed that he could prove the crime was hatched in San Francisco, San Mateo, and Santa Clara counties. He asked that thirteen witnesses be subpoenaed: Frank Goularte, the Pescadero blacksmith; Manuel Goularte, his father;

Dr. C.V. Thompson, the County Supervisor and physician who performed the autopsy; Dr. W.A. Brooke, the County Coroner; Mrs. Elizabeth Nash, San Mateo County Clerk; Josephine Vosti, Widemann's secretary; Mrs. Margaret Harrison, the housekeeper; A.R. Reese, Pescadero resident during the murder; Carl Littlefield, Pescadero resident; M.H. Herman, San Francisco attorney whom Sarah had attempted to call the day before her murder; Captain of Detectives Duncan Matheson; Police Captain Charles Goff; and Policewoman Kate O'Connor.

Judge O'Brien said he would hear further evidence to decide the merit of Herrin's application the following Friday.

The Judge then took a telephone call from Eustace Cullinan, advising the Judge that he would appear on behalf of his clients Widemann and Stirling. Cullinan made it clear that he would absolve his clients and initiate legal action against the accusers. By the way, he added, Widemann was not on his way to Europe but registered at the Bellevue Hotel in San Francisco, prepared for the bitter fight. The false story about Widemann's flight to Europe was "dust picked up by his enemies," according to Cullinan.

To reporters Cullinan said, "The attempt to fasten the crime on Widemann is as funny as a comic opera. The accusation is the result of litigation over the will, which bequested a fortune to Widemann."

Spectators and witnesses crowded the courtroom for the chance to catch glimpses of Widemann and Stirling, while the first three witnesses, Dr. Thompson and the two Goulartes, testified. Thompson contributed no damaging information, but Frank Goularte told of sitting on his porch across the street from the Coburn house with his father late on the night of June 3, 1919. Father and son saw Sarah locking the front door. Later they watched Stirling enter the Coburn home; he waved at them, but Frank Goularte did not see Stirling come out again. Manuel Goularte took the stand and corroborated his son's testimony. There was no mention of Widemann.

Herrin requested warrants be issued for Stirling on the grounds that he could provide a substantial basis for the facts in the case, but the request was denied. It was significant that Herrin mentioned only Stirling, but not Widemann at this time. The matter was put over again, when the remaining ten witnesses would be interrogated.

San Francisco District Attorney Matthew Brady, who wanted badly to be governor, announced that he would launch a thorough investigation to determine which acts were committed in San Francisco. He was prepared to prosecute, and he assigned Policewoman Kate O'Connor and Captain of Detectives Duncan Matheson, who were familiar with the facts, back to the case.

As the hearing continued in Judge O'Brien's court, Carl Eisenschimmel, the handwriting expert for the Police Department, testified. In his opinion the signature on the Sarah Coburn will was a forgery. But Berkeley criminologist Edward Oscar Heinricks said that he had examined the signature, compared it with samples of Sarah's handwriting over fifteen years, and concluded that it was genuine.

Handwriting expert Chauncey McGovern proclaimed the signature a forgery. He had compared Sarah's signature on other documents and concluded that the will was false. Furthermore, he also compared the signature with specimens of Widemann's handwriting given to him by attorney Charles Humphrey and declared that it matched Widemann's writing.

Widemann's chauffeur, J.F. Gooding, said that on June 3, 1919, he was told by Widemann to drive Mrs. Margaret Harrison to San Francisco for a shopping trip in preparation for Sarah's visit to the East Coast. He called for Mrs. Harrison, he said, to drive her back that night, but she told him she wasn't ready to return to Pescadero. Instead he drove to San Jose where he met Widemann, and they went driving with two women. Herrin asked Chauffeur Gooding if he had not testified at the inquest that he was alone in San Jose. No, said Gooding.

Mrs. Harrison contradicted the chauffeur's story. She said that Gooding told her on the night of June 3 that he was not ready to return to Pescadero and that he would call for her the following day.

Loren's nemesis, Carl Littlefield, claimed that on the afternoon of Sarah's murder, Sarah had instructed him to telephone M.H. Herman, a

San Francisco attorney. She wanted Herman to come to Pescadero at once and draw up some trust deeds. Sarah, who was not feeling well, asked Littlefield to keep the call a secret; she wanted to protect the financial interests of her stepson Wally, she said.

The biggest blow to the hearing came when Judge O'Brien rejected Frank Zug's depositions on the grounds that Zug's word could not be accepted.

Judge O'Brien said that in a few days he would announce his decision on whether to issue warrants charging Widemann and Stirling with murder. The warrants were denied when Judge O'Brien said that no testimony had been offered to prove that the murder plot or any part of it had been hatched in San Francisco and that no evidence was offered to show that Widemann was in Pescadero the night of the murder.

Reviewing the testimony of the Goulartes, the Judge accepted that Stirling waved his hand and made no attempt to conceal himself as he entered the Coburn home the night of the murder.

"Case insufficient," said the Judge. "In order to be justified in issuing a warrant for this defendant, the Court must therefore determine from the evidence that said defendant, Widemann, instigated the crime. The deposition of the witnesses failed to show such instigation, so the Court, in order to issue said warrant, would have to indulge in speculation, suspicions, and presumptions. It is a rule of law that suspicion will not justify the issuance of a warrant. Something more tangible is required."

While the 1920's ushered in Prohibition, the Widemann Ranch in Pescadero was the chief landing-point on the Pacific Coast for Consolidated Exporters, Inc.—a million-dollar, Canadian rumruning enterprise. In San Francisco, where he was prosecuting eleven defendants for breaking the Volstead Act, United States District Attorney George Hatfield said that the Widemann Ranch was a principal "port"— more elaborately fortified and furnished with signal lights than a second important landing point at San Luis Obispo. There was a complicated system of signal lights for communication between ships of the rum fleet and landing boats. To prevent attacks by hijackers, a threatening machine gun was mounted on the beach.

During these early years the Elkhorn Saloon and the Nash car were popular in Pescadero. Actors and actresses from the Paul Gerson Motion Picture Company of San Francisco were on location shooting Canadian-Rocky Mountain scenes for a silent feature called "The Timber Pirates". Women wore billowing skirts to hide illegal flasks of booze, while prohibition agents favored fighting the war against booze by chaining "booze-laden autos" to sturdy pine trees.

The commercial properties were changing hands. Carl Coburn sold his store, The Emporium, to A.R. Rease, a Pescaderan who was a resident when Sarah Coburn was murdered. Frank Goularte, the blacksmith, who for a time had owned the lively Elkhorn Saloon, now bought the Hotel Princeton, five miles north of Half Moon Bay. The hotel had already been closed by authorities for "the goings-on" upstairs.

South of Pescadero, Charles Humphrey, the San Francisco attorney who represented the East Coast heirs during the Sarah Coburn will contest, now owned an estate at the Cascade Dairy Ranch, formerly the property of R. E. Steele. Since 1919, when he bought the property from Steele, Humphrey entertained a constant stream of guests.

The Peninsula Farms, a company organized in 1921 and associated with Widemann, purchased Loren Coburn's land. One four-hundred-acre piece was producing forty percent of all the fava beans grown in California. Special machinery was procured for the operation; the beans rolled along a conveyer belt where twenty-five women and girls sorted them into three grades. The Company planned to convert tiny Lake Lucerne at Bean Hollow into a place for summer homes. Trees were planted, boathouses constructed, and a roadway system around the lake was mapped out.

When the ten-thousand-acre Peninsula Farms was placed on the market, it was billed as the largest artichoke and vegetable land in the state. With an investment of one hundred thousand dollars in a new irrigation system, the Company was earning returns which were described as "almost unbelievable." Artichokes, for example, were bringing in twelve to eighteen dollars per crate at fifty crates per acre.

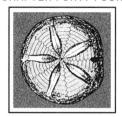

# CHAPTER FORTY-FOUR

# MORE FIRES

After the fire that destroyed buildings on San Gregorio Street, Carl Coburn moved his family into an historic two-story, wooden house known as the Hayward Place, on Pescadero Creek. The structure was built in the 1840's , when Pescadero was a wilderness, with lumber carried into the area by pack mules. An abandoned mill stood nearby. And there was a small house occupied by J.C. Coburn, then about ninety, and his eighty-year-old wife; the couple had recently celebrated their sixty-first wedding anniversary. This Coburn was the last of the nine brothers from Massachusetts.

In the fall of 1924 in the main house at the Hayward Place, a pot of coffee boiled over on a small kerosene stove and started a fire. Flames spread rapidly through the tall, wooden house. Family members, including five children, were in the house when the fire started. With a neighbor's help, the flames were checked from spreading to the house of Carl's parents. The main house was a total loss; nothing in the way of personal belongings or furnishings was saved.

Ten years later, on Saturday night, March 25, 1926, young Claude McCormick was filling his truck with gasoline at the Coastside Transportation Depot in Pescadero. Some gasoline splattered upon a lantern fifteen feet away; there was an explosion, and the building burst into hot flames. The fire spread rapidly; the building next door was consumed, and so was Duarte's Tavern, built about 1890. But the old bar itself was pulled out before the building crumbled.

That night Mrs. Enos's home, where the telephone exchange was located, burned. For thirty years she had been in charge of telephone service, yet she barely had time enough to call the power company in Redwood City to instruct them to turn off the electricity in the village, because the high-tension wires were falling to the street. The first electric light had appeared the year before.

There was still no official fire department in Pescadero. Dozens of Pescaderans, armed with buckets, rushed to Pescadero Creek, filled the buckets with water and tried to douse the fire. They were unsuccessful. In the meantime Traffic Officer Goulson drove the ten twisting miles north to San Gregorio, where he telephoned the fire departments in Redwood City and Menlo Park. Navigating the circuitous mountain roads, they arrived in record time: one hour and eighteen minutes. The firemen dragged the hoses down to Pescadero Creek and started pumping water, which finally put out the fire.

The eastern side of San Gregorio Street lay in ashes. J.C. Williamson, who had been president of the First National Bank of Pescadero, lost his general store. Reduced to charcoal were Duarte's Lodging House, Bennett's Soft Drink Parlor, the Pool Room, Fred Marsh's Meat Market, Frank Goularte's Blacksmith Shop, Rease's Emporium, and Mr. and Mrs. Enos's house where the telephone equipment was located. Half of the business district burned. With losses estimated at two hundred thousand dollars, only partly covered by insurance, the fire was called one of the worst in San Mateo County's history.

The merchants planned to rebuild; and this time there was a consensus that a volunteer fire department had to be formed and adequate fire fighting equipment purchased.

Five years earlier (1921) the old Swanton House had burned down. Mrs. Madel, who discovered the fire, carried her daughter and nephew to safety, while waking up other roomers. The loss was estimated at twenty thousand dollars; all of it was covered by insurance, but the cause of the fire was undetermined. Dr. Thompson, owner of the hotel, announced that he would rebuild, but he never did.

A year before that another fire had nearly wiped out the entire business district of Pescadero. Although some of the merchants did rebuild, there were gaps along the street. The Coburn house and the stables were gone; now the Swanton House was gone, too. Wally Coburn no longer lived in Pescadero, but he was alive. Carl Coburn's house out by the creek had burned to the ground. The Pescadero that Loren Coburn knew was no longer there.

Chris Widemann still lived in Pescadero with his secretary Josie; his "Social Club" thrived, the place where Dr. Thompson and other officials and friends enjoyed the barbecues for which Widemann was famous.

Andy Stirling sued his former boss for thirty thousand dollars and won. The Pescaderans were wary of Stirling and even of the personable Widemann.

The murder became a secret, and the subsequent court cases and related events were not discussed with outsiders. The story itself has been concealed for decades. The murder mystery remains unsolved— just like the many fires that ruined the town. Although the reader has been given plenty of evidence to make a decision, he or she should know that no one was ever prosecuted for the crime.

# FINAL WORDS

*(from villagers and former villagers who were teenagers in 1919)*

"Loren Coburn was a shady character. He did crooked things, like cutting off the road to Pebble Beach. Everybody had it in for him."

"My father told me that Loren was calm, not an aggressive sort."

"Pescadero was the end of the line. Jobs were hard to come by. If you were in with the right clique in the old days, you had your way."

"The rumor was that Andy Stirling murdered Sarah Coburn. She had title to the property; that's why. She would not deed it to Widemann... I thought it was funny Widemann getting in there and getting the property. Everybody was a little afraid of Stirling... But it was possible that Jockey Baker might have done it."

"Dr. Daniel Blackburn was not in on the murder; neither was Mrs. Harrison."

[The murderer] "could have been Jockey Baker or even Kid Zug."

"Mrs. Coburn hid money in the walls. The Quillas found it, and they left Pescadero wealthy."

"There could have been more money than they found in the safe. Widemann paid everyone off with Sarah's money."

The thirty-thousand-dollar lawsuit initiated by Andy Stirling: "The money must have been for killing Sarah Coburn."

About Dr. Thompson: "He put big insurance on his house and then burned it. He collected the insurance."

Carl Coburn's role in the fire at the historic Hayward house: "It was a put-up job for insurance. He [Carl] did not have any money."

"R.E. Steele, the owner of the Cascade Ranch, lost his land to C.F. Humphrey; he buried R.E. on the ranch... "

"My husband and I saw Widemann in Oakland during the Depression. He asked if we could loan him five dollars."

# EPILOGUE

The "Widemann Ranch" became a major landing point for rumrunners during Prohibition.

Chris Widemann married his "secretary", Josephine Vosti. He died of a heart attack in July, 1934 in San Francisco. He was fifty-seven.

San Francisco attorney Charles F. Humphrey, who had represented the East Coast relatives, moved to the beautiful Cascade Ranch, south of Pescadero, in late 1919.

Pescadero saw its first electric light in July, 1925.

In 1927 Carl Coburn was arrested for the second time in Pescadero. He was charged with passing bad checks. Later, he and his family moved away from Pescadero.

In 1928 the Peninsula Farms Company filed for bankruptcy.

Wally, "the boy", Coburn died of pneumonia in San Mateo on November 3, 1933. He was about eighty.

After returning to the East Coast, Arzc Coburn's wife died. He remarried and lived to be well into his nineties, just like his Uncle Loren.

Andy Stirling died in 1939 in Salinas. He was fifty-four.

The Pebble Beach Hotel was torn down to make way for Highway 1.

Pebble Beach is now a state park. A posted sign asks visitors not to remove the pebbles, which are still plentiful.

San Gregorio Street was renamed Stage Road.

The historic Pigeon Point lighthouse remains open to the public for guided tours.

Still isolated, the Pescadero countryside is agricultural, famous for its artichokes and cut flowers.

In 1992 there is an ongoing struggle between developers who want to change Pescadero and those who want the village and countryside to stay as it was in Loren Coburn's time, one hundred years ago.

# ABOUT THE AUTHOR

June Morrall, a native of San Francisco, has had a longtime fascination with the fog-enshrouded coastside south of the big City.

For the past twenty years she has lived in El Granada near Half Moon Bay, and she contributes a regular column to the *Half Moon Bay Review.*

She is a member of the San Mateo County Historic Resources Advisory Board.

Her first book, *Half Moon Bay Memories: The Coastside's Colorful Past,* 1978, is in its third printing.